ZIPPING MY FLY

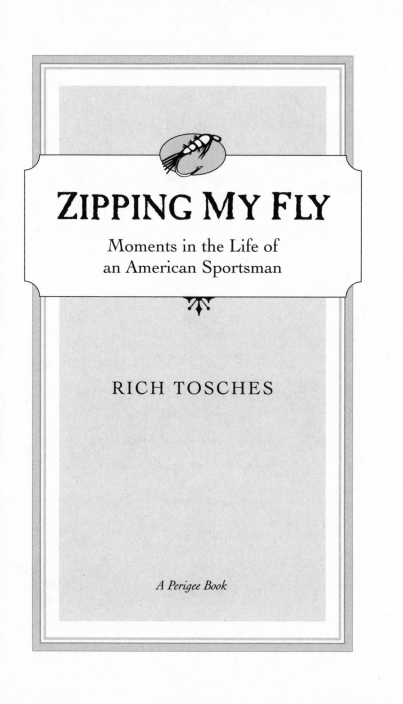

ZIPPING MY FLY

Moments in the Life of
an American Sportsman

RICH TOSCHES

A Perigee Book

A Perigee Book
Published by The Berkley Publishing Group
A division of Penguin Putnam Inc.
375 Hudson Street
New York, New York 10014

First edition: November 2002

Visit our website at www.penguinputnam.com

Library of Congress Cataloging-in-Publication Data

Tosches, Rich.
  Zipping my fly : moments in the life of an American sportsman / Rich Tosches.—1st ed.
    p. cm.
  ISBN 0-399-52819-9
  1. Fly fishing—Anecdotes. I. Title.

SH456.T67 2002
799.1'24—dc21   2002074817

Printed in the United States of America

10 9 8 7 6 5 4 3 2 1

CONTENTS

———

CONTENTS

My First Fly Rod—More or Less

Thirty years ago I first laid my hands on a fly rod, lifting it gently from the red and yellow maple leaves alongside a small creek on a crisp autumn morning in New England. As my small hands felt the perfect balance of the most magnificent fishing rod I had ever seen, my heart began to race and my step quickened, young feet gliding now along the bank of the gentle stream.

Suddenly, as what would become for me a fascination with the art of fly-fishing had barely entered its infancy, I heard a voice coming from my head, a voice

———

that would set the tone for a lifetime of marvelous fishing adventures:

"Hey, you little bastard! Get back here! Put down my fly rod!"

As it turns out, the voice wasn't coming from my head. It was coming from Porky Ferrara, who owned the fly rod and felt a very powerful attachment to it, judging by the way he dragged me down from behind, wrestled the rod out of my hands, and began to choke me.

When he wasn't delivering heating oil to the homes of our small town in Massachusetts, Porky was usually fly-fishing, perfecting the art through trial and error, casting endlessly, trying to master the movements of hand that could send the line and the tiny fly whistling through the air to a precise spot where he believed a wily brown trout or cunning rainbow lay in ambush. Judging from what I saw, he often believed this precise spot was a bush forty feet up on the bank. He would generally celebrate this event by shouting something in Italian that sounded like "Noah good sonamabeech!" which my father told me meant "My, isn't it great just to be outdoors!"

So I studied my mentor, hoping to gain some insight into the science of fly-fishing. And I learned much. I learned about the hatches of insects that send trout into a feeding frenzy. I learned about the importance of stealth when stalking the cautious fish. But mostly, I learned that if you take a clump of moss about the size of your fist and stuff it into your mouth, nobody could hear you laugh.

I've been fly-fishing ever since. The highlight came in 1990, when my employer, the *Los Angeles Times*, approved a sixteen-day trip to New Zealand, where I conducted extensive research into the sport and wrote a 10,500-word account of my trip, a story many literary experts said "contained only seven verbs." The trip ended up costing the newspaper—I am not kidding—$6,875.

It did, however, have a lot to do with my development as a fly fisherman.

On a less positive note, it also had a lot to do with the fact that I don't work for the *Los Angeles Times* anymore.

Nevertheless, in summarizing my three decades of fly-fishing and watching others who are even more proficient in the gentle sport than I am—a group of anglers I would call "all of them"— I can, in all seriousness, say this about my first teacher in terms of his skill, grace, and knowledge of aquatic insects:

Of all the fly fishermen I have met, he was the only one named Porky.

CHAPTER 1

The World Championship: El Mucho Importante Evento

Jackson Hole, Wyoming, is a place of stunning beauty, a valley nestled at the foot of the majestic Grand Teton Mountains, a place of almost magical splendor that the Native Americans called, in very reverent terms, *totonka tanakawa,* or "land of $42 T-shirts."

In the summer, Jackson Hole—the gateway to Yellowstone National Park—beckons the adventurer. And they come in great, sweeping hordes to this land of elk and moose and grizzly bear, all of them hoping for that one special moment when the eyes capture a scene that most wilderness experts believe stays with a person for a lifetime: a guy from Houston in a Denny's parking lot, trying to put his rented, three-hundred-foot Winnebago in the space marked COMPACTS ONLY.

But the most spectacular time of year in Jackson Hole is the fall—when the air tingles with the coming winter and the geese gather for another migration and the aspen trees sparkle and the guy from Houston has now put his wife in the driver's seat as he stands behind the Winnebago with his hands over his head shouting, "OKAY, NOW CUT THE WHEEL TO THE RIGHT!"

And it was during a recent autumn that an event took place that the people of Jackson Hole are still talking about—the seventeenth annual World Fly-Fishing Championship, which attracted elite teams of anglers from eighteen nations, fishermen who spent their own money, leaving their homes in Germany and France and Wales and Denmark and Norway, traveling thousands of miles to this magnificent place with only one thought: "Oops. Maybe I should have told my wife where I was going! Oh well."

Seriously, the World Fly-Fishing Championship was very exciting, leaving the Jackson residents shaking their heads as they thought about Team England's casting skills, about Team Australia's delicate dry fly presentations, about Team Spain's gentle nymphing techniques, about Team Japan's breathtaking fly-tying skills, and mostly, about how they would ever get the smell of cigarette smoke out of Team Germany's hotel room.

The 1996 World Fly-Fishing Championship was held in the Czech Republic, with the gold medal going to the host nation, Team Czech Republic. Team members credited their victory to an intimate knowledge of the Czech rivers, which, during the actual fishing competition, helped them determine precisely where to *placuvas dyenomitovich* or "place the dynamite."

That was just a joke, of course. The World Fly-Fishing Championship is strictly catch-and-release, with no harm coming to any of the creatures involved. The exception would be the Germans' lungs.

For this 1997 World Fly-Fishing Championship, each team consisted of five anglers. There was also a reserve angler, entrusted with many important duties (keeping the cooler filled with beer is just one example), a nonfishing team captain, and a nonfishing team manager. Prior to the competition, the team captain is required to walk out to midfield for the coin toss, where he usually drowns. Then the team manager communicates with his players via a series of hand signals that could mean "cast upstream," "cast downstream," "use a dry fly," "use a sinking nymph," or "bunt."

Scoring was based on a formula involving the number and size of the trout caught, with an "impartial controller" measuring and recording each and every fish. The impartial controller—in more common fishing terms, "the guy who isn't drinking very much and can drive home"—was a professional fly-fishing guide. A professional fly-fishing guide is defined, in strict terms, as a guy who has successfully convinced his wife he is actually making a living and supporting the family in this pursuit. (An "excellent guide" is one who can come home at night, moan about how hard he worked that day, and talk his wife into giving "The Breadwinner" a foot rub.)

Also, the measuring of fish was done in centimeters, a decision made by the international fly-fishing people for two very good reasons. First, it allows a more precise measurement of the fish. Second, and more importantly, this metric system measurement causes the American anglers to blurt out such things as, "Uh, I caught a nice trout that was, uh, let me check my notes . . . 132 hectares. I think." This in turn allows the international fly-fishing people to laugh so hard they emit gas, which causes their rubber waders to expand.

Typical conversation:

SVEN: Jean-Pierre, your waders look as if they may now burst. Was this caused by listening to an American try to figure out how large his fish was?

JEAN-PIERRE: *Oui.* That and how do you say . . . *burritos?*

For more on the scoring system, let's go to the worldwide governing body of competitive fly-fishing, FIPS-Mouche (Fédération Internationale de Pêche Sportive Mouche, which is French and means "International Federation of Guys Who Like Joe Pesci with a Mustache"). Caution: Before you read this explanation of the scoring system, you may want to head for your most comfortable chair and settle in. Although no matter how comfortable you are, after—or perhaps midway through—reading this, you may want to shoot yourself.

Here now, as recorded at the Media Cocktail Party the day before competition began, is the FIPS-Mouche rules chairman, Mr. Jack Simpson:

"You take one man from each team and put him in a group of eighteen anglers. All of the five team members are then distributed evenly and will therefore compete within their own group of eighteen, in that particular time period. So this is very critical. Then we'd be interested in how they change position in terms of these cumulative placings. The team gets credit for each man's placing. If the team is very fortunate in the first round, say, and each of the five competitors places first in each one, the team now has a five and they would be the top team. In the second period they compete again and the individuals carry over their placings. So does the team. Tiebreakers are points and number of fish and finally, the largest fish, until the tie is broken. Those who are rewarded are those who show the greatest consistency. If one fellow gets 50,000 points in one period and no points in the others—or an eighteen—yet someone else had greater consistency in all five, he would win. Like a one and then an eighteen in four of them. He can't win. It's a very fair system. As for the wading portion, we're looking at the 200-meter beat plus the 20-meter buffer zone in which no one can fish. These will be physically marked with signs such as A, B, C, D, one through eighteen, and so on."

Some would say the oddest thing about this 6-million-word explanation by Mr. Simpson was that all stuff about the one and the eighteen and the 50,000 points.

Although if you ask me, the oddest thing about his long explanation was the fact that I had only asked him if FIPS-Mouche was handing out any free-drink tickets.

CHAPTER 2

The Grand Marshall Was a Carp

As all anglers know, there are things to be done before any fishing can take place. For some anglers, there are worms to be dug up. This is best accomplished with a heavy shovel on a grassy area, preferably at night after your neighbor has gone to sleep and will not, in strict angling terminology, "be watching his front yard."

There are hooks to be sharpened, too, so that the barb will more easily penetrate a fish's lips and result in a higher catch ratio. More importantly, a sharp hook will be easier for your doctor to remove from your nose, thus freeing up more time for his more serious and life-sustaining work, such as golf. (That was just a joke. Doctors have far more important things to do than play golf. Keeping the office stocked with a complete set of 1973 *Reader's Digest* magazines and hiring a receptionist strong enough to hold you down and rifle through your wallet for an insurance card would be two examples.)

But no matter what type of angler you are, there is one thing that always precedes a day of fishing. That, of course, would be the parade.

The World Fly-Fishing Championship parade took place in downtown Jackson Hole, and at the risk of sounding melodramatic or elevating this event to some sort of mystical plateau, let me say this: Not only did it make me teary-eyed, but it also caused two of my ribs to snap and forced a huge mouthful of root beer to come out of my nose.

Heading up the parade was a band riding on a float, playing the emotional strains of the seventeenth-century French concerto *Behinez Bunchous Guylairre Fishez,* or "Behind Us Are a Bunch of Guys Who Are Going Fishing." As the parade kicked off and the band turned the corner onto Main Street, a roar went up from the several hundred onlookers, mostly residents of Jackson Hole who had long anticipated this moment. From the sidewalks they waved and cheered and hooted and hollered as the anglers drew closer, which gives you some idea of the magnitude of this event and, of course, the overwhelming loneliness that comes with living in Wyoming.

The first contingent of anglers to appear was Team Canada, its athletes marching proudly and silently, and their very appearance shouting out to the world, "We Are Canadian Athletes!" In other words, they were all wearing skates and cups and had no front teeth. I'm kidding. I love Canada. And, like most Americans, I fervently hope that one day they can break away from the United States and forge their very own country.

Behind Team Canada was Team France. Here I must caution you that I plan to bring into play all of my immense writing skills to conceal the highly suspenseful ending of this book, which will come, in literary terms, near the end. So I won't say very much at this moment about Team France.

Let's move on to the third group of fly fishermen in the parade, Team Italy, which marched right behind the eventual winners.

Damn.

Anyway, leading Team Italy was Edgardo Dona, a master angler who has developed his vast array of skills despite having only a few hours a week to practice. The rest of his time is spent in another pursuit, one he practices relentlessly, day and night, indoors or outdoors, in summer or in winter: laughing.

Edgardo Dona got off the airplane in Jackson Hole laughing. His baggage appeared on the airport carousel, which also made Edgardo laugh. During the week a member of Team Finland told a joke to his teammates and Edgardo laughed very hard, even though he does not understand a word of Finnish and believed the punch line of the joke to be, "And the uncle says, 'A carp? Not when I have two fields to plow with Bob's lamp!'"

With Edgardo were teammates Edoardo Ferrero, Mario Altora, Carlo Baldassini, and Pierluigi Cocito. Pierluigi, as you know, is a traditional Italian name which means, literally, "Let's take Luigi for a little walk on the pier." (That, obviously, was just a stupid joke and was not meant to offend any specific group of people. But just in case, I will now move to a new house and take different routes to work each day.)

Team Italy wore striking Armani suits for the fishing parade, the apparel reflecting all of the classic Armani trademarks: pleated trousers with cuffs and jackets with a full cut and gently falling lapels that accent the torso. And, of course, a four-by-four patch of unprocessed wool near the shoulder, where you can stick artificial flies.

As the parade continued through Jackson Hole, the passion we all shared for fly-fishing grew ever more evident even as the eight-hundred-foot-long Winnebagos on their way to Yellowstone were forced to stop and were backed up all the way to Utah. Near the Teton Kids Clothing Store (TODAY ONLY: T-SHIRTS $34.50 OR TWO FOR $85!) Team Belgium was strutting its stuff, its anglers looking sharp in their brown-and-white suits made entirely from the most well-known native Belgian fabric: waffles. Team members Marc David, Francis Lambinet, Alain Gigot, Alain Colonval, and Jean-Michel Grégoire smiled and waved behind their banner, which carried Belgium's national motto, which, loosely translated, goes like this: "We Know Our Names Are French. It's a Long Story."

Next came Teams England and Finland—the English looking magnificent in that typical English rumpled sort of way and the Finns shielding their eyes and cowering behind very dark glasses, almost as if they hadn't seen the sun in six months.

They were followed by Team Poland, led by master angler Marian Mozdyniewcz, who came to Jackson Hole with a lofty goal in mind: catching a trout longer than his name.

Next through the streets of Jackson Hole was Team Spain, its members—their instincts honed from years of similar street gath-

———

RICH TOSCHES

10

erings in their own country—looking nervously over their shoulders as they walked, wondering when parade officials would release the bulls.

Team Norway followed—the clear favorite should ice fishing break out. Then came the Australians—hopping, with all their fishing equipment in pouches on their stomachs. Team Slovakia was next, a group of men whose country has been torn by terrible conflict for the past decade but has now, thankfully, recovered to the point where everyone goes fly-fishing. Then came Ireland and Wales, two teams that with their mere presence signaled there would be some serious beer drinking.

New Zealand was next, whose members of the fly-fishing team accurately reflected that nation's population makeup. By this I mean the team consisted of one human and four sheep. Then came Team Germany, which, as previously mentioned, went through cigarettes like Michael Jackson goes through noses. The fly-fishing parade was no exception. It seemed odd, then, that placed directly behind—or downwind of—Team Germany was a U.S. Forest Service float containing Smokey the Bear, who today is still in counseling.

Second to last in the lineup was Team Japan, which would not perform all that well in what Fédération Internationale de Pêche Sportive officials refer to, in technical terms, as "the fishing part," but the Japanese anglers did look resplendent in their dark suits and matching red ties. And they have about forty-eight thousand photographs to prove it.

And finally came the Americans. The streets echoed with the roars of the crowd as Team USA lit up, faces aglow with the joy only a fishing parade can offer. And as the cheers grew louder, they walked slowly and soaked it up, from their cowboy hats to their cowboy boots, four men and one woman on their home turf now, five Americans who would, at the end of this competition—in the shadow of the inspiring Grand Teton Mountains—make the following statement in the international arena of fly-fishing:

We'd be dead last if Team Japan had not shown up.

CHAPTER 3

Hail to the Herring

Let your mind wander back to the summer of 1996, when the greatest athletes in the world gathered in Atlanta for the very dramatic Olympiad that had a lot of Roman numerals with it. Recall that golden moment at the opening ceremonies when perhaps the greatest athlete ever, Muhammad Ali, raised a trembling hand with the flame of Olympia and lit the torch that would, for sixteen days, light up the world.

Now whack yourself in the head several times with a heavy pot and try to forget it, because the opening

———

ceremonies of the seventeenth annual World Fly-Fishing Championship were not like that at all. For starters, Muhammad Ali was unable to carry the torch into the Jackson Hole rodeo grounds, having made a previous commitment in the area of choosing new linoleum for his huge kitchen.

To be honest, there was no torch at all for these opening ceremonies, which was somewhat of a disappointment to the fans and a huge disappointment to Team Germany, which had planned on using the torch to light their cigarettes and now had to settle for a more tedious method of lighting up: briskly rubbing two Frenchmen together.

This is not to say the opening ceremonies for the fly-fishing event were not dramatic. As a matter of fact, as the national anthems blared over the loudspeakers and the fly-fishing teams marched in behind their flags, I felt a lump in my throat. As it turns out, a hatch was taking place on the nearby Snake River and the "lump" was actually a giant mayfly. This in no way diminished the excitement of the opening ceremonies, although it did diminish my appetite for the next two days.

First to march into the arena was Team Slovakia, accompanied by their heart-wrenching national anthem, which I will now try to sing to you: "Da-da, da-da-da daaahhhh!" The anthem is entitled "Als Slovaken Wordsjk" or "We Think the Anthem Would Be Better If It Actually Had Words."

Slovakia was followed by the anglers from Team Spain, who entered the outdoor rodeo arena bearing centuries of tradition in the science of fly-fishing, traditions that at that moment had each member of the team thinking about just two things: When do we get to kill the bull, and who gets the ears?

Team Wales entered next, marching to their spirited anthem,

"Even Our Shorts Are Tweed." The rest of the nations followed then, Team Canada marching to its anthem ("O Canada"), just ahead of Team Australia ("O Australia"), Team Finland ("O Finland"), Team Norway ("Hail to the Herring"), and Team Italy (theme from *The Godfather*).

Anyway, when the teams were in place in the arena, the mayor of Jackson Hole stepped to the microphone and bellowed, "There you have it, folks. The very best fly fishermen on the whole dol' garned planet Earth! Welcome to Jackson Hole, Wyoming, and now I say, 'Howdy, pardners!' which is our way of saying welcome."

On a somewhat negative note, "Howdy, pardners!" sounds almost exactly like the Italian words for "I, personally, plan to sleep with each and every one of your wives while you are out fishing." The reaction from the anglers of Team Italy was swift and direct. That's right; they laughed so hard they blew the cameras out of Team Japan's hands.

"We are very pleased and excited that you have chosen our community for this competition," the mayor continued after allowing the Japanese anglers to retrieve their cameras and pound some of the dirt out of them. "If you haven't noticed it already, we are in a very unique and spectacular part of the world."

(Specifically, a part of the world in which during the nine months of winter, guys can get so lonely they begin giving human names to the elk. The most common one is Debbie.)

The mayor—who was now getting angry at all of my idiotic interruptions—went on to tell the international field of anglers, "What you probably don't know yet is that the people here are as warm and friendly as the scenery is beautiful."

(On a personal note, I imagine that if a bunch of tourists gladly

———

ZIPPING MY FLY

15

handed me $42 for a T-shirt with a picture of a moose on it—a T-shirt that came to my store at the cost of $1.39, thanks to a lot of hardworking eight-year-olds on the night shift in Malaysia, well, I'm guessing I'd be pretty damn warm and friendly, too.)

The mayor closed by saying, "And so, once again, I'd like to say 'Howdy, pardners!' and welcome to Jackson Hole."

The Italians laughed again.

Although this time, they were also keeping a pretty close eye on their wives in the bleachers.

The anglers then filed into the bleachers to watch a Wild West show. As they got to their seats, they demonstrated many different forms of resting on the seats. Highlighting this International Exhibit of Sitting Down were the anglers from the Czech Republic, who—I am not kidding about this—each spread one Kleenex-brand nose tissue on the metal seats and then rested their buttocks on this piece of paper. Feeling an explanation was in order, I asked master angler Jozef Lach to explain the tissue thing.

Here now, are his actual words: "Seats dat hat . . . or maybe I say *hot* . . . and we are not want hot pants for our suits. And they one seat . . . are dirty, either."

What Jozef was saying, obviously, is that the Czech Republic anglers, including himself, had sat on their hats, which didn't work out so good, so now they were trying Kleenex. Further, their behinds were hot for some unknown reason and at least one of them had had "an accident." This, in turn, forced the rest of the team to inhale ether.

Out in the arena—and here I will use the formal rodeo terminology, so please try to stay with me—a cowboy was chasing a small cow. He finally caught the cow by throwing a clothesline rope around its neck, and then, to make sure it did not get up and run away before he could get the barbecue fired up, he used both of his hands to tie the little cow's feet together with more clothesline rope.

At this, the anglers stood and roared their approval, the loudest roars coming from the anglers of Team Australia, who not only use this same roping method to tend their cattle, but also to get a wife. I am just kidding, of course. Australian men don't use *both* hands to tie a prospective wife's feet together. They need one hand to hold the ninety-eight-ounce can of Foster's.

And as the calf struggled to break free, the Japanese, the master fly-tyers in the international field, were on the edges of their seats, too. They seemed to sense they might never get a better opportunity than this to gather material for their special fly (a tan caddis with a Hendrickson wing)—the main ingredient of which is the hair from the ass of a small cow.

The ceremonies concluded with an emotional dance by Native Americans, members of the local Flathead tribe. Interpreting their dance as best I could, I surmised that the dancers were calling on the spirits to watch over the anglers, for the weather to cooperate, and for Jozef Trnka of Slovakia to buy a vowel.

The opening ceremonies came to an end and then, with the start of the tournament drawing ever closer, the best fly fishermen on the whole dol' garned planet Earth filed out of the stadium—the Canadians hopeful, the Americans confident, the Poles eager, and the Italians staying between their wives and the mayor.

CHAPTER 4

Das Fish—Big Wet?

As the days of pomp and banquets and parades and cocktail parties continued, I was reminded of an old saying in competitive international fly-fishing circles, one coined by the Germans: *Evn We Beeren. Ltesen Go Fasen,* which means, literally, "Even we can't drink any more beer. Let's go fishing."

And so, eventually, the best anglers in the world prepared for a day of angling. Officially, it was known as a practice day, with the results not counting in the Official Scoring System understood only by Einstein and, now, Jack Simpson of FIPS-Mouche.

———

The anglers would practice on the Greys River, some fifty miles from Jackson near the Idaho border. (During the actual tournament, the anglers would fish one day in Idaho, forcing officials to explain to foreign anglers the difference between a "brown trout" and a "potato.")

Anyway, the trip to the Greys River would involve loading the fly fishermen onto school buses for the long drive, which prompted the anglers to ask many questions. Examples would include "What is this Greys River?" (Team Slovakia); "How long does such a trip take?" (Team Spain); and "What is a school bus?" (Team Finland).

The loading operation was to begin at 5:30 A.M. in the parking lot of the Snow King resort, forcing the anglers to set their alarm clocks for 5 A.M. Except for Team Germany, which set its alarm clock for 3 A.M. so each team member could smoke a quick pack of cigarettes before climbing onto the bus.

At 5:15 A.M. the place was a zoo. By this I mean the Welsh were searching for their fishing rods, the New Zealanders were running around looking for their waders, and Team Poland was trying to get out of its room without waking the polar bear, the leopard, and the monkeys.

In the lobby of the Snow King, one-hundred world-class fly anglers milled about, all of them now wearing waders and carrying their fly rods, along with long-handled landing nets.

They drank a lot of coffee, too, forcing them to pile into the men's room in great waves. And not to get off the subject, but if you missed the fly-fishing event and want to see thirty or forty guys smoking cigarettes and standing around the urinals with their rubber pants and suspenders pulled down to their ankles as they hold fishing nets in one hand, well, quite frankly, you'll have to wait for the next Alabama State Fair.

———

RICH TOSCHES

20

At 5:30 A.M. the anglers had moved outside, awaiting their bus assignments. Volunteers with clipboards scurried about in the darkness, shouting out instructions in English, which was good news for the eight or nine anglers who understood English. For the others, there was a bit of confusion. Example:

BUS ASSIGNMENT PERSON WITH CLIPBOARD: Okay now, Olav Syvers-
    braten, Norway; Jaroslav Barton, Czech Republic; and Bernard
    Marguet, France, please report within five minutes to Bus No. 6.
OLAV SYVERSBRATEN (in Norwegian): I am fishing with Clara Bar-
    ton, the famous American nurse?
BUS ASSIGNMENT PERSON: No, that's JAROSLAV Barton. You are in
    Group P.
JAROSLAV BARTON (in Czech): No thank you. I just went.
BERNARD MARGUET (in French, with his mouth full): Anyone want
    a handful of snails?

This went on for about thirty minutes in the darkness—Finns talking to Spaniards, Italians talking to Germans, Poles talking to the New Zealanders, the Irish packing their waders full of pota-toes in case another famine broke out.

In general, no one understood anything, which was in accor-dance with FIPS-Mouche Official Competition Rules Article 16, subsections 16.3–16.5, which clearly states: "Landing nets must not exceed one hundred and twenty-two (122) cm/forty-eight (48) inches in overall length, fully extended. Further, the com-petitor may only stand while netting the fish, but if he has asked the controller to net the fish, the competitor must remain seated."

This first subsection, standardizing the size of landing nets, was instituted to thwart all that "Mine is bigger than yours!" bravado so common among anglers. The second portion of the so-called Netting Article, the one regarding sitting down and standing up, prevents an angler from netting his fish while lying on his back, kneeling, squatting, or sitting down in the fast-moving river.

(Footnote: That rule is currently being challenged by attorneys for Fédération de Pêche Sportive Poland, the hardy Poles claiming a long tradition of netting large trout while bobbing up and down in a river, often three or four anglers at the same time, all of them floating in the deep water with only their hats visible. Although historians believe this may be not so much "tradition" as it is the result of "all of them reaching across the boat for a sandwich at the same time.")

Back in the parking lot, the carefully orchestrated division of groups or "Angling Units" was nearly complete, with anglers shuffling around in a smooth and orderly fashion, or as the Spaniards often say, *likez fumar drildejo las Chineze,* or "like a Chinese fire drill." Somehow, I found my way to one of the school buses and climbed aboard for the ninety-minute ride to the Greys River. My bus contained the following ancestry: French, Italian, Spanish, Slovakian, German, Irish, Welsh, Belgian, and Australian.

And that was just the driver.

Seriously, the bus contained twenty-six men from fourteen nations. And one woman, Team Canada's Kathy Ruddick. As the yellow school bus chugged toward the river, the men talked about all the things you'd expect from sophisticated, mature, international fly-fishing anglers. Topics included the latest fly rods and reels, the excitement of fishing a new river, and mostly, of course, who had the coolest lunch box and whether Hywel Morgan of Wales, who was sitting in the same seat as Kathy Ruddick, would catch "cooties."

I found myself sandwiched on a bus seat between Poland's Artur Raclawski (which means, literally, "Arthur should really trim his toenails") and Ulrich Schneider of Germany. Now, I don't know how many of you have ever been crammed onto a school-bus seat between a Pole and a German, but let me say this about my experience: I spent ninety minutes sweating profusely, waiting for some kind of invasion to begin.

This did not happen, of course.

Although at one point I complimented the German on his very nice fly-fishing vest.

He smiled and, in his broken English, said, "Tanks!"

And the Polish guy dove under the seat.

We arrived at the Greys River at 7:30 A.M., which was, on the biological clocks of the anglers, 12:30 P.M. in France, 4:30 P.M. in Spain, and January in New Zealand. I got off the bus at the first stop along the river, partly because I wanted to watch the meticulous Japanese anglers, Junzo Ishino and Kunihiko Tsuzuki, but mostly because I had tired of the conversation between Raclawski and Schneider.

Actual highlight that I have on tape:

RACLAWSKI: I am have good fish maybe how?
SCHNEIDER: Das fish! Big wet.

Anyway, Ishino and Tsuzuki waded in and with long, sweeping casts began testing the water. The ninety-minute bus ride, combined with six cups of coffee, had me involved in some hydro-research myself. Although my research had brought me not so much into the Greys River itself but rather into the bushes about fifty feet away. (Startling scientific conclusion: Peeing into the wind can make your shoes wet.)

I emerged from the bushes and walked along the bank, stopping to watch the two master anglers. They caught a few trout and soon came ashore for a break. I showed them my notebook and tape recorder and then we introduced ourselves. After a lot of bowing, they smiled and gave me the nickname Mr. Jurinishoko, which I believed meant Mr. Journalism but later learned means "Mr. Urine Shoe."

When they stopped laughing—it was now about noon—Junzo said this: "I am the student. Mr. Tsuzuki is the teacher." This became apparent over the next few hours, as Junzo would set the hook too quickly on a gently rising trout and pull the fly away from the fish, or occasionally allow the line to hit the water with a hard splash, spooking the timid trout.

And each time Mr. Tsuzuki would walk over and smash Junzo's hand with a wooden ruler and send a note home to his mommy and daddy. Once, he made the trembling young man scratch out the words "I will not snag the shrubs!" one hundred times. In the hard dirt. With a stick. I am just kidding. It was only fifty times. With his finger.

Seriously, the two often stood side by side, the master showing the promising young fly angler the intricacies that separate world-class fly-fishing from, say, bass fishing. Example: Fly fishermen can recognize hundreds and perhaps thousands of insects in the pupal, larval, and adult stages. Bass fishermen, meanwhile, can sometimes recognize their own house. (Generally by the color of the propane tank in the front yard. If that doesn't work, they go to the next step in house identification—counting the number of wheels on it.)

Anyway, Mr. Tsuzuki had figured out that the trout were feeding on emergers that rise from the stream bottom toward the surface. And now, to emulate this movement with his artificial fly, he was skillfully raising his right arm high over his head along the pine tree–lined banks of the river. And I think you can imagine the result. That's right, Mr. Tsuzuki's right armpit was virtually moisture free and smelled like pine trees.

No, what really happened is that he hooked a trout on nearly every cast, the fish following the emerger from the bottom and attacking as it neared the surface—just like the classic movie *Jaws*. Except, of course, as I stood on the bank of the Greys River, I did not have to listen to actor Roy Scheider scream, "Get out of the water!" several thousand times.

Anyway, Mr. Tsuzuki caught about a dozen trout, and later, as the sun set behind the mountains, summarized his day: "I have good luck small fish, no big luck fish," he said, echoing my own thoughts. "Big fish, I think, other fish. Yes? Emerger is good today. Tuck cast. Emerger. Next day, who know? Much change. Small fish. Good."

And somewhere, Dan Quayle was smiling.

CHAPTER 5

Bite My Kiwi, Mate

The second most interesting thing about New Zealand is this: There are 3.3 million people in the country and 70 million sheep. (Here we will play a game of Make Your Own Joke. Although I strongly suggest a punch line containing the words "Wyoming" and "Sadie Hawkins dance.")

Anyway, the *most* interesting thing about New Zealand is the fly-fishing. As a staff writer at the *Los Angeles Times*, I was fortunate enough to convince my boss in 1990 to send me to the South Pacific at the *Times*'s expense for fourteen days of spectacular fishing. This played a major role in my development as a fly fisherman. On a slightly less positive note, it also played a major role in why I no longer work at the *Los Angeles Times*.

The journey began with a thirteen-hour flight from Los Angeles to Auckland, during which I had enough time to write down the entire list of highly successful Kevin Costner films. Then the plane actually took off.

Because of a complex series of time zones, we left California at 11 P.M. on Thursday and arrived in Auckland at 2 A.M. on Monday, a month before we had departed from Los Angeles, I think. I do know this for sure, however: We crossed something called the International Date Line. (Which is also what Woody Allen crossed when he began going out with his teenage Korean stepdaughter.)

After a sleepless night in an Auckland hotel (the hotel was fine, but because of my intellect and curious nature, I stayed up all night flushing the toilet and watching the water swirl around *counter*clockwise), I boarded another flight to the New Zealand capital of Wellington. This is where the government makes all its major decisions, such as whether the national anthem should contain words other than "baaaahhh."

From there, another short flight brought me and Bill Hoyt—a fellow fly angler from California whom I met in the Auckland airport—to the South Island town of Nelson, where we rented a car. From the car-rental agent: "You're in luck today, gentlemen. We've got you a Bluebird!"

I did not know what he meant by a bluebird, but I did know this: If history does indeed repeat itself, my brother was going to shoot it in the eye with a BB gun.

As it turned out, a Bluebird is a car—more or less—that is as popular in New Zealand as, say, our Ford Explorer. (The main difference is that when the road surfaces get above seventy-five degrees, its tires do not explode and Firestone lawyers do not come running out of the bushes.)

Soon we were off, me getting comfortable behind the steering wheel, which was on the right, or "wrong" side of the dashboard, and gunning the Bluebird down the left, or "wrong" side of the road. On my left, Bill knew he was in good hands and quickly settled into the passenger seat with visions of gigantic trout dancing in his head. And eighteen pairs of rosary beads wrapped around his fingers.

Just minutes into the drive, I swerved into the right lane, then swerved back into the left lane and panicked when I saw the enormous, bright headlights of a truck bearing down on us from the left. Fortunately, these "headlights" turned out to be Bill's eyes. (He must have been homesick and missing his wife and kid because right after that he kept mumbling "Sweet Mary and Joseph!" over and over again.)

Our first stop was the Lake Rotoroa Lodge, nestled in the Nelson Lakes National Park. As we approached the lodge we crossed a bridge over the Gowan River. We got out and Bill spotted an enormous brown trout resting on the gravel in the clear water. When we reported this to the lodge owner, Bob Haswell, he calmly replied: "Oh. That would be Trevor, the pet trout." (This made it much different than being in New Jersey, where, when you report seeing something huge resting on the bottom of a river, the typical reply is: "Oh. That would be Vinny, the rat-bastard.")

Trevor, we were told, had called the water under the bridge his home for a few years, and despite frequent attempts to fool him with a fly, he had never been caught. I even made a few skillful attempts myself, most of which consisted of kneeling on the bank, holding a net behind my back, and saying softly, "Heeere, Trevor!"

Anyway, for three days Bill and I fished with guide Zane Mirfin, a twenty-year-old New Zealander who had an uncanny ability to spot trout from great distances, often in fast-moving and riffled water. This made Bill and me think at times that he was, well, different from us. The sharp beak and the white feathers growing from his head only reinforced this feeling.

Seriously, we crept behind Zane along the majestic rivers for three days. When he spotted a huge trout he would stop, crouch lower, and back up toward us. Then, using his skill and experience with these wild and majestic trout, he would formulate a strategy to catch them, often starting with pinching out the burning fuse on the stick of dynamite I had just lit.

The first such stop came on the Rolling River, with a five-hundred-foot rock cliff on one side and a thick, tropical jungle on the other. Once in position, Bill made a perfect case to a six-pound brown trout, which moved to his nymph, inhaled it, felt the sting of the hook, and immediately headed downstream toward the, uh, the Straits of Magellan or Cape Horn, or maybe it was Cape Cod. (In school I was never very good in geometry.)

I kept casting as Bill worked the monster back toward us, his fly rod bent nearly double. After about ten minutes Zane slid a net under the massive trout and let out a shrill, piercing whooping sound—which I believed was some sort of New Zealand celebration whoop until Zane pointed out that my woolly bugger was stuck in his ear. (That, of course, was just a joke. It was a large pheasant-tail nymph that must have had quite a sharp hook, judging by the way Zane chased me into the jungle with a big stick.)

RICH TOSCHES

Day after day, Zane showed an amazing ability to spot giant trout where Bill and I saw only rocks and gravel. This made Zane laugh and mock us. Although he mocked us in that good-natured, I-would-still-like-a-big-tip sort of way customary among fly-fishing guides. At the head of one riffle he paused, and we knew he'd seen a trout. Because there would be many others—and also because it was another opportunity to mock us—Zane let us walk up to where he was standing and asked if we could see the fish.

Bill could not, even though his eyes were still pretty big, not having recovered yet from several of the so-called driving incidents on the way down. (Example: Because everything was opposite, I drove around and around a rotary on a highway so many times and at such a high rate of speed that when I finally stopped, Bill staggered out and tried to pin a tail on a donkey.)

I could also not see the huge trout, even though Zane kept pointing at a spot just behind a big rock and, in his funny accent, shouting "Roight thair!"—which is New Zealand, meaning "Great! I am guiding Ray Charles and Stevie Wonder!" Finally, Zane grabbed my fly rod, stuck the tip deep into the water, and suddenly a large pile of gravel, perhaps some thirty inches long, exploded and swam away. I felt ridiculous and looked sheepish. Being in New Zealand at the time, I think you probably know what happened next.

That's right, Zane apologized, bought me flowers and candy, and asked what my sign was.

We caught eighteen enormous trout in those three days and then said good-bye to many new friends and hit the road again. During the farewell, as we climbed back into the Bluebird, Bill had a lump in his throat. I thought it was the emotion of saying good-bye, but it turned out to be handful of Prozac and sleeping pills that he was trying to swallow. This appeared to make the passenger experience much more enjoyable for him. Occasionally he'd wake up and shout, "And I'll miss you most of all, Scarecrow!" then go back to sleep. But other than that everything went okay.

After a few hundred miles of driving we pulled into Cedar Lodge, north of Queenstown. There we met guide Owen King, who would later look at a fish and say, "Aye, now that's bein' a wee fat one, he was!"—which as best I could tell meant either (a) it was a small fat trout; (b) it was a fat small trout; or (c) Owen had gotten a plate of bad mutton and was now hallucinating.

In the morning Bill and Owen and I climbed into a helicopter piloted by lodge owner Dick Fraser. We soared just over the tops of the New Zealand Alps at 100 mph, twisting and turning in a heart-stopping flight as Dick laughed and made jokes about crashing. Still, Bill insisted this was a lot better than going around and around that rotary in the Bluebird.

After thirty minutes we landed alongside a gorgeous stream and began a memorable day of fishing under the shadow of Mount Awful, a towering mountain that got its name because when the sunlight hits it just right it looks like Rush Limbaugh in a Speedo. (Even when it becomes volcanic, it spews less hot air than the chubby radio guy . . . and I hereby vow not to make any more Rush Limbaugh jokes.)

Anyway, Owen operated the same way Zane had farther north—stalking large trout, then backing off and saying things to the anglers that they didn't understand because everyone in New Zealand sounds like Prince Charles on crack.

At the first stop, however, Bill connected with an enormous rainbow on a dry fly, the massive fish rising to the surface and in-

---

RICH TOSCHES

haling the caddis like Rush Limbaugh sucking down a double cheeseburger.

Oops.

When Bill set the hook, the small stream erupted in spray as the fish took off, peeling the fly line and then much of the backing from the reel as Bill and Owen sprinted downstream after the trout. I followed as best I could with a notebook, jotting down important notes for my *Los Angeles Times* story, such as: "fish runs downstream; can't see legs; wonder if trout have knees? I'm spending $7,000 of someone else's money to go fly-fishing for two weeks! ha-ha-ha!"

During the battle I interviewed Bill, who was having one helluva time fighting this fish and running along a boulder-strewn bank while at the same time telling me to shut up and trying to kick me. I tried to interview Owen, too, but quickly became confused ("Aye roon, he roons . . . makes for woon eeeeepic bottle, now don't it?) and ran farther downstream, thinking it would be easier to interview the trout.

After twenty minutes, Bill had the monster near his feet and Owen netted it, although the giant trout still battled bravely even when he was in the net, desperate, it seemed, to disappear back into the waters of his native creek before Owen could say anything indecipherable to him. Trout, as many of you know, do not have hands and therefore are unable to scratch their heads, as Bill and I did whenever Owen said anything to us.

Later it was my turn, with Owen backing up toward me, pointing to a spot about fifty feet upstream, and saying, in an excited whisper: "She's a monster, and moight be fadin' on droys so we best jest be watchin' hare for a meenut!" I looked at Bill and he just shrugged his shoulders. (Then, when I turned my back, he wrestled the Bluebird keys out of my pocket, threw them into the river, and laughed like a lunatic for fifteen minutes.)

Fifteen minutes later Owen allowed me to—and here I use the complex, scientific expression for this behavior—"actually try to catch a fish." On my first cast a twenty-five-inch trout rose to the fly and took it. I responded as I had done so many times in twenty years of fly-fishing: I panicked and jerked the rod back over my head in a savage, violent motion that broke the line. As he turned and walked away, Owen began quietly mumbling more New Zealand words, this batch sounding like "Aye, we got ourseeelves one doom-sheet heah, na' don't wee?"

About an hour later, on my next try at one of New Zealand's giant brown trout, I laid a dry fly fifteen feet upstream of a huge, dark shadow that Owen said was a "beeg brune," whatever the hell that is. This time, when the huge trout sucked the small caddis off the surface, I set the hook calmly and the battle was on! The trout ran upstream. He ran downstream. He ran through the briars where a rabbit couldn't go, although those might be song lyrics. The point is, this fish was huge and was giving me quite a beating.

Then—and I'm not kidding about this—the fish did the most amazing thing. It powered its way *into* the opposite bank and disappeared, with the line still screeching off my reel. Seconds later the fish leaped from the water, twenty-five feet upstream, the hook still in his jaw and my line still running straight into the bank. The fish, we discovered later, had gone into a water-filled tunnel under the bank, a tunnel worn by the flowing water, and had come out of the bank upstream. Owen was shrieking all kinds of things in what I believe was the native language of people from Denmark. What he wanted to do, I eventually understood, was get to the opposite bank, cut my line, grab it as the fish pulled it out of the upstream hole, and then *tie the two ends back together* so I could continue to fight the giant fish.

I suggested he hold the rod while I wade into the narrow creek and beat the fish senseless with a heavy stick and get my $1.25 fly back.

The debate became moot a moment later, however, when the line broke and the fish swam free.

"Neevah' seen enytheeng loik that!" Owen said. "He wint roight for that 'ole in the bink. Moosta knewn it was theere! Moight smart bloke he woos!"

I said "Right!" as I plucked a $1.25 fly out of the patch of wool on his vest and put it in my own.

More than a decade later, I still think about that day.

Specifically, I still wonder what the hell " 'ole' in the bink" means.

CHAPTER 6

515 Miles and No Trout
(Let's Be Frank)
Nightmares in Wyoming

You don't have to travel halfway around the world to get confused by fly-fishing. I can honestly say—and excuse me if this sounds like bragging—that I've been puzzled and bewildered by fly-fishing in Alaska, Colorado, Montana, Wyoming, and the Dakotas—North Dakota, South Dakota, East Dakota, and even West Dakota.

I think it's because I have not become really scientific about the sport, like, say Frank Plucinsky of Pennsylvania, who is featured in an ad in the February 2001 issue of *Fly Fisherman* magazine. In this ad there's a big photo of Frank. Under his chin are the words: "My diary has a record of every hatch I've fished for twenty-six years." This makes him different from me in the sense that under my chin are more chins.

The ad, for Sage fly rods, goes on to say: "If it flies, flits, or flutters, trout fisherman Frank Plucinsky knows it by name (in both Latin and English, of course). In fact, he knows life on Pennsylvania's Tulpehocken Creek so well, he can tell you when the caddis are on just by the blooming of Virginia bluebells that grow along its banks."

I do not even know what Virginia bluebells are. Although my cousin Tony, who lives in Roanoke, told me he once had a really bad case of Virginia blue *bal*—uh, let's just say he was single and lonely.

The point is, Frank has written down detailed descriptions of every insect hatch he has encountered in the past twenty-six years of fly-fishing. I, by way of comparison, cannot remember where I was last night or, at this moment, my middle name. So I cannot compete with fly fishermen such as Frank. (Which is why avid fly fishermen sometimes refer to dynamite and a heavy stick as "the great equalizers.")

I'm just kidding, of course. I am a big proponent of catch-and-release. Well, you know, I would be if I could ever *catch*.

Take a recent fly-fishing adventure I took with my equally inept fly-fishing friend Mike Anton. Like most Americans, we caught no trout during that particular six-day period in May. What made us different, perhaps, is that we drove 515 miles during that time period along some of the greatest trout streams in Colorado and Wyoming, often stopping, getting out, putting on our waders and vests, and *trying* to catch trout. We fished up to ten hours each day, stopping only occasionally to down a quick meal of

---

Prairie Dog McNuggets. (Did I mention we spent part of the trip in Wyoming?)

Anyway, here now, just like Frank Plucinsky's diary, is a summary of that particular trip.

Wednesday, May 10

2 P.M.: Stand near window in newsroom of newspaper where I work in Colorado and shout, "Look, it's Jimmy Hoffa!" When everyone runs to window, I sneak out back door, meet Mike, and leave on fishing trip. As we drive away, boss Cliff has sent team of reporters to ask the twenty-five-year-old sandwich truck driver across the street if he is Jimmy Hoffa.

6:30 P.M.: Arrive in Laramie, Wyoming.

7 P.M.: Check out Laramie cultural district.

7:08 P.M.: Depart Museum of Rodents.

7:30 P.M.: Stroll into Buckhorn Saloon, look at patrons, become frightened.

7:45–9 P.M.: Mingle nervously with locals. Gain valuable insight into technique for field dressing an elk using only your teeth and a bottle opener.

9:30 P.M.: Find cheap motel, go to sleep.

10 P.M.–7 A.M.: Have nightmares about Wyoming. In worst one, I am a sheep.

Thursday, May 11

10 A.M.: Arrive in remote Saratoga, Wyoming. Sign reads POPU-LATION 1969, which is, as it turns out, also the fashion year residents are stuck in.

11 A.M.: Wade confidently into famed North Platte River.

11:15 A.M.: Return to truck. Wring out pants and shorts. Put on waders.

11:30 A.M.–3 P.M.: Serious fishing in "Blue Ribbon" river. Catch nothing. Blame this on wind, inability to match the hatch, and unbelievably finicky trout. Local anglers we encounter believe repeatedly slipping on moss-covered rocks and falling into the river may also have played small role.

Friday, May 12

6 A.M.: Determine North Platte River has no trout. Set sights on nearby Saratoga Lake. Local fly-shop owner says lake contains lots of five-pound rainbows and browns. We ask how cold the lake water is and whether a man could "freeze to death if he repeatedly fell into it." He asks why that would concern us. We tell him to mind his own business.

6 P.M.: No trout in Saratoga Lake, either. Return to car. Wring out hats. See more local anglers, clutching their midsections, pointing at us and laughing in what appears to be some sort of "Wyoming welcome."

Saturday, May 13

6 A.M.: Return for another shot at Saratoga Lake. I am swayed by fishing partner's argument that it seemed "easier to swim back to shore in the lake than in the fast-moving river."

10 A.M.: Return to car. No trout. Crowd of local well-wishers now estimated at three hundred. They send up wild roar as we wring out our hats. We climb into truck and hit the road, vowing to return "when the fishing improves."

Noon: Leave Wyoming, cross into Colorado. Sign reads WELCOME TO COLORADO. PLEASE WIPE YOUR FEET BEFORE ENTERING.

2 P.M.: Arrive at famous Blue River. Desperate to do better, we take out insect screens, turn over rocks, and carefully examine the aquatic creatures we find.

4 P.M.: Sure beyond any reasonable doubt exactly which insects trout are not feeding on.

6 P.M.: Arrive at South Platte River near town of Hartsel, which combines Native American words *har* ("Who") and *tsel* ("took all the trees?"). In South Platte River, actually see huge trout rising to insect hatch that I'm sure Frank Plucinsky has made forty pages of notes about.

7 P.M.: No trout.

Hate Frank Plucinsky.

CHAPTER 7

The Drivel Runs Through It

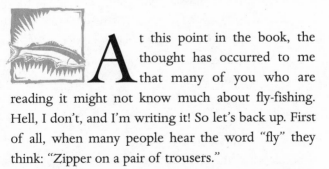

At this point in the book, the thought has occurred to me that many of you who are reading it might not know much about fly-fishing. Hell, I don't, and I'm writing it! So let's back up. First of all, when many people hear the word "fly" they think: "Zipper on a pair of trousers."

(Monica Lewinsky takes this sentiment so far that when she hears "fly" she starts whistling "Hail to the Chief.")

Anyway, if I wrote about an actual weekend I had in May of 1997 and began by saying I spent most of the time with my fly stuck in a tree, a lot of people would think I was somehow dangling by my crotch from the branch of a pine tree, screaming all day. This, of course, was not the case. It was a cottonwood, and I stopped screaming after the fourth hour, knowing I might need my strength when I "cut myself down."

And if I told you during that same weekend my friend Bill Vogrin kept getting his fly snagged on his own hat, you'd probably think: "Well, that's better than Bill Vogrin's fly getting stuck on YOUR hat."

Bill, Mike Anton and I were, of course, fly-fishing—a sport often defined as a jerk on one end of the line waiting for a jerk on the other. It is a sport every bit as frustrating as golf. The main difference is that in golf you don't spend all day in soaking-wet pants. Unless you start missing three-foot putts with $50 bets riding on them.

Anyway, the site of our adventure that weekend in 1997 was the Arkansas River near the Colorado town of Salida (town motto: "Don't Call Us Saliva.") We were there because of the hatch of the caddis fly, which sends the usually wily trout into a feeding frenzy—like Rush Limbaugh when he hears the buffet is closing in twenty minutes.

The secret to catching a lot of fish during this hatch is a stealthy presentation of the fly, the ability to "read" the water, and, of course, bringing enough dynamite. (The exciting part comes when the stunned fish float to the surface, or "rise.")

As a bonus, after about the fifth or sixth detonation you generally find yourself with a long stretch of river all to yourself, the other anglers—especially the ones without OSHA-approved BA-99826 hearing protection devices—having staggered up the riverbank, furiously pounding their hands against their ears.

(Director Robert Redford's decision to ignore this particular form of fly-fishing was my only real complaint with *A River Runs Through It*.)

Upon arriving at the river that day, we spent about thirty minutes rigging up our rods, a process in which a leader is connected to the fly line. The other end of the leader is then connected to a fly. This fly with its very sharp hook is connected to the tippet. And, as I remembered a moment later when I took a step backward and plummeted over a steep embankment, the thighbone is connected to the hipbone.

I was the "expert" of the group on this day because once, while fly-fishing in Alaska in September of 1982, I hooked a sixteen-pound rainbow trout. Technically I did not "catch" this gigantic trout because I was practicing my casts inside the lodge and the trout was mounted on the wall—although that in no way diminished the thrill.

(Alaska is a super-friendly place, but I sensed the lodge owner was becoming slightly irked after I "set the hook," yanked the fish off the wall, beat it with a heavy stick, and demanded he take a photograph of me holding it up.)

Back along the Arkansas River, I spent a few minutes with my friends and fellow journalists, going over the three key rules:

- Remove the hooks from your nose promptly, before tetanus sets in.

- If you actually catch a fish, you will be banned from any further fishing adventures with the group.

- The best defense against libel action is ignorance.

Soon we were actually fishing, waving the fly rods wildly over our heads like Florida voters trying to punch the hole near Al

Gore's name. And shockingly, we actually began catching trout. Bill, who is from Kansas, scored first, bringing a fourteen-inch brown trout into his net and shrieking, "Goll-eeeee! It are a swordfish!"

Then Mike caught one, which caused him to spew out an eighty-five-word sentence that included twenty-six words no one else had ever heard of. (Mike writes for the *Los Angeles Times*.)

The most memorable moment, however, came when I hooked a real whopper. After a lot of yelling and screaming, I got it onto the bank, removed the hook, held it, and posed for a quick photo.

Even today, when people come to my house, they almost always gaze toward the mantel above my fireplace and ask the same question:

"Is that a picture of your nose?"

CHAPTER 8

Dances with Morons

Now that we've covered the basics of the sport, let me tell
you about one of the greatest
fly-fishing trips I've ever been on. It was a trip to Montana, the state made famous in *A River Runs Through It*.
In that movie, Brad Pitt is forced by his domineering
father to try something he apparently doesn't like and
is not any good at: acting.

Anyway, the trip took us to the Bighorn River, which
required us to drive six hundred miles. It was a spectacular drive, except for one barren, treeless stretch called eastern Wyoming (motto: "The Land That Scenery Forgot").

Among the actual Wyoming highlights:

- The Interstate 90 exit for the towns of "Banner/Story." (In the Sunday edition, a gigantic headline trumpeted: CLYDE DRESSES UP SHEEP, AGAIN!)

- Montana has the famed Little Bighorn battlefield, but Wyoming—and I'm not kidding—has the "Fetterman battlefield." As I understand it, General Fetterman's cavalry battled valiantly but in the end lost all of their chicken soup and a third of their matzo balls.

- Chugwater, home of "Wyoming's Famous Chili." Chugwater—and trust me on this—allows you to get lunch AND gas all in one stop.

- The Crazy Woman River. The Crazy Woman runs through eastern Wyoming—then makes her way to Connecticut, where she keeps breaking into David Letterman's house.

Anyway, eventually we got through Wyoming and onto Montana's Crow Indian reservation. There we stopped and asked directions to the Bighorn. If you are lucky, as I was, you are given a proud American Indian name such as Soaring Eagle.

(Although that particular name was apparently already taken. So, after having to repeat the directions to the river to me seven times because my mind kept wandering, the woman in the store bestowed upon me another proud American Indian name: Dances with Morons.)

Fishing headquarters was the village of Fort Smith, an old cavalry outpost named for the former *Playboy* centerfold who married an eighty-nine-year-old Texas billionaire with heart problems. I'm talking, of course, about model Anna-Nicole Smith (Indian name: Digs for Gold).

For two days we drifted in a small boat that contained just the basics: oars, an anchor, and a bewildered Cuban boy named Elián González. No, really, we caught enormous trout from our drift boat. In one stretch of the river, near sunset, we watched thousands of big trout sipping midges. The last time anyone had seen that many things rise to the surface of a river was along the banks of the Hudson River in New York on April 14, 1974—three days after they had "squealed on Vinny."

Seriously, in one four-hour period on the Bighorn, I caught and released more than fifty large trout. It was a trip I will never forget. If you ever get up that way, stop in the general store.

And tell the woman that Dances with Morons sent you.

CHAPTER 9

Vail to the Chef

hen you think of Vail, Colorado, you probably think of world-class skiing and rich people. And not just regular rich people, but the high-and-mighty kind of rich people, the kind who drink beer from a glass and have someone else wash their poodles for them. I, by way of comparison, drink my beer straight from the can—usually in a crowded bar when the guy who bought it turns away for a second. Oh sure, this method occasionally results in a mouthful of soggy cigarette butts, but I believe that's a small price to pay for free beer.

Also, I wash my own poodle. He seems to like that. And he usually does okay until the Kenmore Ultra Fabric Care Model 80 kicks into the spin cycle, at which time loud, screeching, whining noises emanate from the machine. (I think it needs a new drive belt.) Then, so the little guy doesn't get pneumonia, I take him out of the washer and get him right into the dryer. Making sure, of course, to first remove my cat, Fluffy.

The point is, Vail offers some terrific fly-fishing along with the famous skiing. Although you probably want to conduct these activities on two separate days, unless you're an idiot and like to be swept downstream in the Eagle River while clutching a fly rod in one hand and furiously trying to unbuckle your ski boots with the other, which CAN happen if you're in a hurry and not thinking. (On a more positive angling-related note, before I hit the deep pool, I managed to spear a fourteen-inch brown trout with my ski pole. I know what you "fly-fishing purists" must be thinking, but relax. I released him!)

Anyway, recently my thirty-year friend and fishing companion, Rob Bresciani, who lives ninety miles away from me in Boulder, Colorado, called. Rob and I have fly-fished together in tiny creeks in our home state of Massachusetts and in raging salmon-filled rivers in Alaska and in lots of places in between. This includes a place in Colorado called the Roaring Judy, although we were drinking a lot of beer that weekend and I don't recall if that's a river or what we called the bartender when she saw Rob relieving himself on the pool table. (I do, however, remember him yelling "Whoa! One-ball in the corner pocket!")

And the bond between us is a strong one, forged by laughter and time and, mostly, by the fact that no one else really likes us.

Anyway, Rob's wife and daughter were out of town for the

weekend, and he missed them terribly. The sadness in his voice was plainly evident on the phone when he shouted: "I've got the whole $%^&*# weekend to myself!"

That evening I somehow found myself in the town of Golden, home to the Coors brewery, which makes a terrific beer and, as a bonus, regularly dumps tens of thousands of gallons of beer sludge into a nearby river and kills all the fish. (Coors motto: "Making Everything Go Belly-Up, Including You After a Couple of Six-Packs.")

Anyway, coincidentally Rob showed up in the same parking lot at just about the same time, and after stuffing all of my fly-fishing stuff into his Suburban, we found ourselves headed west through the Rocky Mountains toward Vail and the Eagle River, two boyhood friends together once again, laughing and talking about the same silly, juvenile things we talked about thirty years earlier as teenagers. That's right: swollen prostate glands and erectile dysfunction.

We cruised into Vail and marveled at the castles nestled into the mountains, seasonal homes of people who have worked hard and achieved the American Dream. "Rich $%^&*(#@" was how we put it. Here is an actual story that tells you all you need to know about Vail:

If you're like me you've got an extra $45,000 in your pocket right now and are asking yourself the obvious question: "Do I make a long-term mutual-fund investment directed at the future educational needs of my children, or do I get that beautiful four-weight Orvis rod I've been looking at and a new sport-utility vehicle to put it in? (I've got my eye on that new, sixty-seven-ton Ford Exhibitionist.)"

And while I don't want to influence your decision, I spent four years at Marquette University in Milwaukee, Wisconsin, remember approximately six days of it, and have no intention whatsoever of spending money so my kids can drink Pabst Blue Ribbon beer, bowl, and have as much sex as I did.

Okay, I lied. But I'm serious about the Pabst and the bowling.

Anyway, another way to spend that $45,000 would be—I'm not kidding—to purchase one of the fifty parking spaces in an exclusive underground garage in Vail. It's called the Golden Peak Passport Club, a name chosen during secret balloting by the members of Vail Associates, who narrowly rejected the other fine suggestion for a $45,000-a-space parking garage: Chuck's U-Park-It.

The $45,000 spaces are on Tier 1. Tier 2 parking is slightly less expensive and does not offer all the services you get on Tier 1—such as the glossy, just-licked-clean-with-my-own-tongue look the Tier 1 parking attendants give your tires.

The fifty spaces are just about gone now, and a price hike is being considered. From David Corbin, vice-president of development for Vail Associates: "We'll keep raising the price incrementally as we feel the market will bear."

Or, to paraphrase P. T. Barnum: There's a Golden Peak Passport Club member born every minute.

Oh, and this: Vail Associates will return the club members' $45,000 initiation fee to them.

In thirty years.

And I don't know about you, but I'd like to be there the day all those 110-year-old guys drive into the garage to pick up their checks.

So anyway, Rob and I cruised into—and out of—Vail, and as the sun began to disappear beneath the towering peaks of the Rockies, we pulled up alongside the Eagle River some forty miles farther west. The surface was alive as big brown trout feasted on a late-day caddis hatch, and we scrambled from the truck in anticipation of a spectacular evening in the river. We rigged our fly rods, climbed into our waders, and—here I will let the magic of words paint the picture for you—"felt the cool water pressing against our big, middle-aged asses."

Then the storm hit. Bolts of lighting. Monstrous claps of thunder. Heavy rain and hail. The fish stopped feeding. And suddenly an evening filled with so much wonder and anticipation just moments earlier had been magically transformed into two idiots standing in a river, waving long graphite poles over their heads in a savage lightning storm, their waders starting to fill up with hail. I do not know if God is a fly fisherman. But if He is, I am guessing (a) He has some really nice clothing from the Patagonia company; and (b) He was up there that evening, looking down on two anglers and laughing so hard that holy water was coming out of His nose.

We squished our way back to the truck and headed for the nearby town of Edwards. We purchased a small bottle of tequila and two limes and talked about how much we'd grown up and matured over the past thirty years. (We used to buy a big bottle of tequila and no limes.)

Then we checked into a motel, talked about the meaning of life, and drifted off to sleep with that wonderful feeling in the pits of our stomachs, the feeling of anticipation fly fishermen get knowing a glorious day on a fly stream awaits them. Although the feeling in my personal stomach was mitigated somewhat by the large chunk of lime I had swallowed while gulping down tequila from a plastic Motel 6 cup.

The morning dawned crisp and clear, and we headed downstairs for the free continental breakfast. Thanks to me and the empty backpack I brought into the dining room, this also became free continental lunch and free continental dinner. Fact: The Columbia Sports Dayhiker Model 200 can accommodate fourteen bagels, six blueberry muffins, and five apples, with plenty of room on top for a large, fluffy Motel 6 towel.

Our first stop was the local fly-shop, where, in the finest tradition of fly-fishing, we handed over the obligatory $35 and walked out with a handful of flies the shop owner swore the fish were "really hitting." We got back into the truck and headed for the river; the morning air was so still and quiet we could hear the fly-shop owner laughing four blocks away.

We arrived back at the Eagle River shortly before 10 A.M., located a beautiful set of riffles and a deep hole Rob's friend had given him directions to, and kicked off what would be a memorable day that would involve the following phrases:

"Got one!"

"They're really on the prince nymphs!"

"That $%^&*# cow's face is coming back up on me!"

I will save the explanation for that last actual statement, made by Rob, for the end of this section, thus ensuring you will read through the next thirty or so pages.

Anyway, we positioned ourselves in some fast water and went at it. Rob nailed a nice brown on his third cast, a prince drifting near the bottom triggering a savage strike. I had my eyes on a rising trout about fifty feet downstream, thirty years of fly-fishing experience telling me a sizable fish was taking tiny emergers just below the surface, and that in all likelihood, I would fall into the river twice trying to get into the perfect casting position, and once I got there, the son of a bitch would be full and would go deep and begin a Gandhi-like fast.

Amazingly, this did not happen.

I only—I am not kidding—fell into the river ONCE.

RICH TOSCHES

After wringing out my shirt, I watched the big trout rise again. I laid a perfect forty-foot cast just upstream, and stunningly, he took the tiny fly and the war was on. And what a war it was. The most incredible part came when I pressured him into some quiet water, and he responded by invading Czechoslovakia.

Actually, I had the eighteen-inch brown whipped in about three minutes, the great fish indicating that he'd had enough by rolling on his side. Waving a small white towel at me seemed to confirm my belief. I released him with a flick of my forceps and he swam slowly into a quiet pool, where another trout joined him. The second one moved close and seemed to be taunting him about having been caught by an idiot carrying a backpack full of stolen muffins, but perhaps I was reading too much into the whole thing.

Rob was into a nice trout upstream, but lost the fish after he had eased it to within a few feet of his waders. He lost several other fish that way on this day, perhaps because of the tiny hooks, or his landing technique—which involved throwing his fly rod into the bushes, grabbing the silk-thin 6X leader, and shouting "I've got you now, you little bastard!"

By noon we'd hooked some twenty trout, releasing all of them either after the fight or, in Rob's case, during it. Then, despite the twenty pounds of free hotel food on my back, we decided to take a break and get something to eat up the road. We settled for the El Cantina roadside Mexican food truck, which is, as promised, getting us to Rob shouting "That $%^&*# cow's face is coming back up on me!"

I ordered a couple of pork burritos, and Rob, who is Italian, shook off the disappointment that came when a puzzled-looking Lupe told him they did not have lasagna. He pointed to the chalk-board menu and asked, "What's this?" She said something we did not understand, and moments later Rob had two of whatever "that" was on his plate. As it turned out—and I swear I am not kidding about this—he was eating tortillas filled with, according to a nice Hispanic man sitting next to us at a picnic table near the truck, "meat from a cow's cheek."

Rob said it was delicious.

However, an hour later, back in the Eagle River, he started looking funny.

Then he burped. It was real loud, indicating either gastrointestinal problems or a methane explosion in a nearby coal mine.

He solved the debate for me about ten minutes later when he lurched toward the riverbank and made the following announcement: "That $%^&*# cow's face is coming back up on me!"

Despite his medical problems, Rob stayed in the river, a flyfishing warrior if there ever was one, a dedicated and driven man in the mold of John Wayne. And while I don't recall the great actor ever eating a cow-face burrito, I have to admit that I haven't seen all of his movies.

Anyway, we caught a dozen more trout over the next three hours, I with a No. 20 Adams and a No. 22 emerger behind it, trying to focus on the tiny flies while constantly glancing over at Rob, who kept belching and talking about the cow face. Similar things have happened to Rob and me for thirty years, evoking great howling laughing fits. I will write about other amazing adventures we've shared—like fishing in Alaska with a guide who saw a grizzly bear, pulled out a .44 magnum handgun, and promptly shot a hole in the bottom of his boat. But here I'd like to say this: I hope Rob and I have thirty more years of pounding the rivers together with our fly rods.

And if you're ever in Colorado and happen to see us fishing, drop by and say moo.

———

RICH TOSCHES

I'll Be Comin' 'Round the Mountain (When I Get This Hook Out of My Ear)—Pikes Peak

Among my favorite places on earth is a reservoir called North Catamount. Catamount means "mountain lion," so I guess one of my favorite places on earth is North Mountain Lion, whatever the hell that means. Anyway, the reservoir is nestled among towering pines and dazzling aspen trees at an elevation of ten thousand feet, on Pikes Peak in Colorado. Pikes Peak, as many of you probably know, was made famous in 1893 when Katharine Lee Bates climbed to the top, was overwhelmed by the sight of "purple mountains' majesty" and "fruited plains," and was moved to pen the lyrics to the classic American song "Me and Mrs. Jones (Got a Thing Goin' On)."

Okay, it was "America the Beautiful."

But the point is, none of that lovely history prepared me for my first—and only, barring some kind of miracle medical breakthrough involving an antiscreaming pill—trip to the summit of this beautiful mountain. The only good news from the trip is that it uncovered for me this gem of a reservoir teeming with large cutthroat trout.

Anyway, the trip to the summit of the 14,110-foot mountain began when I met Nick Sanborn, executive director of an annual road race to the top called the Pikes Peak Hill Climb. I climbed into his white Chevrolet Suburban for what I believed was a leisurely drive of about two miles, to a meeting place on the Pikes Peak Highway with another person who would take me the rest of the way.

Nick greeted me with these actual, comforting words: "I've raced this road so many times there's no thrill anymore in scaring myself. But I do like doing it with people like you in the car."

Then he laughed and stomped on the gas pedal. As we drove around hairpin turns on the side of the mountain, I asked Nick general questions about the race and the adventure it presented for the drivers, questions that went to the very heart of auto racing. An example would be: "Hey, Nick! Guess who?" as I clamped my hands over his eyes.

Midway up the mountain—and here I use the common Pikes Peak Hill Climb expression—"where the pavement ends and the years of intense psychiatric care begin," Nick turned me over to the man who would take me the rest of the way: veteran race-car driver Roger Mears.

Although Roger had raced this course many times, this one would be somewhat more difficult than usual because of many uncontrollable natural factors such as loose gravel, patches of ice, the passenger repeatedly diving over the console and leaning on the brake pedal with his hands, the passenger giving Roger quite a beating with his rosary beads. Things like that.

Let me say something here. I don't know exactly what mode of transportation Katharine Lee Bates utilized to get to the summit of Pikes Peak in 1893, but if Roger Mears had driven her there, we'd all be singing a very different "America the Beautiful" today, starting with these lyrics:

> *O beautiful, for spacious skies,*
> *All I can say is 'Yowsers!'*
> *Roger drives like he is nuts*
> *And now I need new trousers!*

Anyway, Roger was also driving a white Chevrolet Suburban.

(Footnote: If you're thinking of buying a white, 1997 Chevrolet Suburban, I'd strongly suggest not getting either of the white ones with the gigantic stains on the passenger seat.)

Suddenly we were on the actual racecourse. "Here's where A LOT OF PEOPLE GO OFF THE SIDE!" Roger shouted about a mile up the gravel road as he slid the Suburban sideways into a corner at 50 mph. Directly beneath us, at a distance of what I estimate was 1,458 miles, straight down, was the tourist town of Manitou Springs, Colorado.

My stomach tightened as I was gripped by the most common fear a person gets in this situation: plunging over the side and landing on a gift shop in a Chevrolet Suburban, smashing everything in the store except the "You Break It, You Buy It!" sign.

For the next seven minutes I was flung around in the vehicle like a rag doll, screaming and pulling on my own hair, which is bright red and made of yarn. As Roger slid the large vehicle to the edge of the cliff several hundred thousand times—I lost the actual count at 156,987 when I was struck in the head by my own foot—we had a lovely conversation about race-car driving and the thrill inherent in the sport. It went like this:

ROGER: I took the bark off the trees right there. I think it was in the '79 race!

ME: Oooooooohhhhhhhh!

ROGER: Right up here we . . . WE DROP THE RIGHT FRONT WHEEL OVER THE SIDE so we can line up for the straightaway!

ME: SWEET JESUS, MARY, AND JOSEPH! PLEASE FORGIVE ME. I THOUGHT SHE WAS EIGHTEEN!

ROGER: That drop there is about 1,400 feet. But you gotta' GET THE TIRES WITHIN SIX INCHES OR SO OR YOU'D HAVE TO BACK OFF THE GAS PEDAL!

ME: SANTA MARIA!

(I don't know why, but often, when I see death looming, I begin shouting out the names of Christopher Columbus's ships.)

On we went, though, sending up gravel and clouds of dust as we roared past actual areas called:

Devil's Playground: This was our lucky day: The recess bell had just rung and Satan was on the seesaw.

Bottomless Pit: Hikers say when the light hits this rock formation just right, it looks exactly like Oprah Winfrey in a buffet line.

Boulder Park: This one is named for the Colorado town made

infamous by the JonBenet Ramsey case. We were slowed here as the park ranger negotiated with our attorneys over taking a lie detector test, then made us give him handwriting samples.

Soon—and I cannot overemphasize just HOW soon—we made it to the summit. We got out, stretched our legs, and gazed at the exact same view that moved Katharine Lee Bates more than a century earlier.

Well, Roger did.

I was in the backseat, curled up in the fetal position, working my way through the names of Ferdinand Magellan's entire fleet. Which was pretty embarrassing. Although the real embarrassing part was the last mile of the ride.

Roger made me sit on newspapers.

However, as I may or may not have mentioned earlier, it was on this day that I saw water shimmering in the distance. Because we went by the sign at the turnoff to the reservoirs at what I estimated was seven hundred miles an hour, I knew the sign said either NORTH SLOPE RECREATION AREA or NOFT SBOBTH RIOPRECI ANIA.

One of the three reservoirs, NORTH HOUSECAT or whatever it's called, is a hidden gem, a mecca for fly fishermen. I say "mecca" because the first day I made this pilgrimage I watched in a solemn, respectful way as a man put down his fly rod, faced toward the east, dropped to his knees, and let out a low, religious-sounding wailing noise.

Turns out he'd hooked his ear with a No. 14 Parachute Adams.

But since that day I've spent countless hours walking the shoreline of the majestic reservoir, matching wits, as they say, with huge, cruising cutthroats. (Last week I took an eighteen-incher into the Bonus Round, finally bowing out when I failed to correctly answer the question "Who is on Mount Rushmore?" I got Millard Fillmore and Dan Quayle, but couldn't remember the other three.)

The first trip brought me and Dr. Jerry Thompson to the shores of the reservoir. Jerry was my brother-in-law back then. Today, he is not my brother-in-law. Because I'm a mature, forty-six-year-old man, I won't get into all the details of who did what to whom, or who got what in the divorce settlement, or in any way allow even a hint of bitterness to creep into a humorous book about fly-fishing.

Although I will say this: I bet when Stephen King slides back his "chair" and stands up after writing a book, he does NOT have milk-crate lines on his ass.

Anyway, Jerry and I hiked about a mile from a parking area, across the dam, and into the forest before finding a trail to the water. Immediately we saw large trout rising, sipping mayflies from the surface. I rigged both fly rods—Jerry is a pediatric surgeon and likes to save his hands for more important things than tying knots in tippet; an example would be cranking open a pickle jar when his wife hands it to him—and we started casting. In the clear mountain water we watched the trout come to the flies from a long distance, the anticipation building up, to use the old expression, "like Bill Clinton's blood pressure on Intern Interview Day."

For about half an hour the trout came to the flies and turned away, sometimes even bumping them with their nose before rejecting them. Then I dropped a tiny mayfly emerger about eighteen inches behind my dry and suddenly fishing was as much fun as watching a television news anchorperson when the TelePrompTer breaks down. A twitch of the dry fly would bring a trout in for a close look, and then they would gulp the emerger and the fight was on. After my fourth nice trout, Jerry, who had wandered about fifty feet down the shoreline, shouted, "What are they hitting?"

"The mayfly!" I shouted back with great excitement. "Right on top, just like you're doing. Just stay with it."

I like Jerry a lot. But frankly, I had no idea how many trout were in the reservoir and wanted to catch thirty or forty of them before giving away my secret. I'm like that. It's why hardly any of my friends will ever go fishing with me a second time. (The brightest ones don't even go the first time.)

Soon, though, I had added the emerger to Jerry's arsenal and the day became, to use one of his favorite expressions, "more fun than removing a child's malfunctioning spleen."

During the cutthroat frenzy, I began seeing an occasional larger fish cruising the shallow coves. Unlike the cutthroat, these fish had deeply forked tails and I knew I was looking at mackinaws, or lake trout. They weren't like those unbelievably huge lake trout of the Northwest Territory lakes of Canada, the kind the anglers have to shoot with a gun, whack over the head with a log, and then drag up onto the beach with winches (I loved that particular episode of *American Sportsmen* back in the early seventies, especially when Curt Gowdy got into a frenzy and accidentally whacked the guide on the head with the log), but these lake trout were big enough—twenty inches and more.

They weren't, however, interested in the mayflies drifting above them. I looked closer and began seeing small suckers hunkered down along the bottom. That's what the lakers were interested in. So I switched to a brownish streamer fly, added a split shot, and began bumping it along the bottom. The first lake trout came savagely to the fly, actually creating a wall of water with his snout—much the same way you figure Barbra Streisand does when she takes a dip.

I set the hook and line sizzled from my reel and I let out a tremendous whoop.

"What do you have?" Jerry shouted.

"Uh, just another cutthroat," I replied. "Nothing to see here. Go on about your business."

He's pretty smart, though, and walked right over and saw the twenty-four-inch lake trout at my feet, and I had to give him my last brownish streamer. Had to tie it on, too. Then I carefully revived the magnificent fish and watched him swim away.

Let's talk for a moment about this catch-and-release stuff.

I haven't eaten a trout. Ever. I don't eat fish of any kind, except for an occasional can of tuna. (Porpoise is good, too, but I hate all the squeak-squeak-squeak noises they make when you're trying to get them into the boat.)

Seriously, I think all fish taste, well, fishy. I mean, what other food do people talk about that way? "Try this kind," I've been told a hundred times. "It DOESN'T TASTE LIKE FISH." And I wonder what kind of an idiot, if he wanted something that didn't taste like fish, WOULD EAT FISH? Pork. Now there's something that REALLY doesn't taste like fish. Or a steak.

Or anything from McDonald's, including the filet o' fish, which is made from the employees' recycled paper hats.

And then I get this: "You go fishing all the time, BUT YOU DON'T EAT THEM?"

Then I ask them if, when they go bowling, they have a great desire to EAT THE SMELLY RENTAL SHOES, ready to draw the obvious correlation as to why I don't need to eat the fish I pursue.

Unfortunately, when I ask that last question, most of the people I hang around with indicate that they DO enjoy eating the rental shoes, and my argument is shot to hell.

The point is, I am a true catch-and-release guy.

Although once in a while, if a friend knows I'm heading for the river again and asks me to bring back a big trout for his barbecue grill, I will almost always return to town, drive directly to his house, open my Coleman cooler, and hand him a bowling shoe.

Jerry and I must have caught sixteen or seventeen trout that day, a few lakers but most of them brilliant cutthroats—"the lawyers of trout," as they're known. There have been perhaps fifty more trips back to North Pussycat Reservoir over the years, mostly resulting in terrific memories of action-filled days.

But every once in a while, for reasons known only to God and Bill Gates, who thinks he's God, I get shut out. Blanked. Skunked. (Twice I've returned and had to give myself a bath in tomato juice. Then I tried to cross the road in front of my house, got flattened by a truck, and stank up the entire neighborhood for three days.)

Okay, that last part never actually happened.

But I've had days on this reservoir in which the fish are cruising and eating vorashus . . . vorraciou . . . A LOT, putting away mayflies, caddis flies, and even pop flies, although I may be thinking of a New York Yankees game I watched on TV last night. Anyway, on some of these days nothing artificial seems to interest them.

Which is, by the way, the same reason Michael Jackson doesn't get a lot of dates these days.

I'd gone to twelve-foot leaders and 7X tippet. I'd changed flies as many as two dozen times, searching for a single fly or combination of tiny dry and nymph that might trigger a strike. But each attempt brought the same result. A trout would rise to the bug, hesitate, and turn away. It was maddening. On one of these days, I had perfectly matched the small callibaetis hatch—and if you're a devoted fly angler you've had this happen to you, too—and was staring like a madman at my artificial fly, surrounded by the real insects being plucked from the surface by feeding trout, when suddenly, and quite startlingly if you're really focused, the artificial fly FLEW AWAY. And you realize you were NOT watching your fly, which is no longer floating and has disappeared in a gigantic swirl three feet to the right.

And it is at this time, and only this time, that respected clergy members—including Pope John Paul himself in the Vatican's monumental Fly-Fishing Edict of 1994—agree that it is okay to shout "Goddammit!"

CHAPTER 11

The Painfulliness of It All

The rematch.

I spent two weeks preparing to resume my battle with the trout of North Catamount Reservoir. I'd read articles in fly-fishing magazines, checked and rechecked my equipment, and even dropped the obligatory $35 on the counter of my local fly shop. (I think the guy gave me a strike indicator for my $35, but I'm not sure and, frankly, don't care anymore.)

The magazine article I studied during this two-week training program was in the September 2001 issue of *Fly Fisherman*. It's the one with the cover photo of President George W. Bush fishing with his father off the coast of Maine. The president has a striper fly embedded in his earlobe and, in the accompanying story, talks about the "painfulliness" of the incident.

Anyway, here's what the actual article, entitled "Fishing Small Dry Flies," had to say:

> During most small-fly hatches, trout position themselves just below the surface and eat the minute insects like whales eating plankton.

Which explains why once, in 1994, I hooked a twelve-inch brook trout that stripped all the fly line from my reel, then all the backing, then blew air out of a hole atop its head, and beached itself, after which a crowd of screaming and crying Greenpeace people tried to push it back into the water. I'm not kidding!

Anyway, the actual story goes on to say:

> Holding near the bottom and rising to the surface when an insect enters their window isn't efficient enough. This would be like sitting in your living room, having a bowl of popcorn in the kitchen, and for each piece of popcorn you ate, having to get up and make the journey to the kitchen.

I have often caught trout that were feeding in this manner, using a method I pioneered myself. First, I leave a large Coke and a box of Milk Duds on the shoreline. Then, when the trout come out of the water and grab the snacks, I leap out of the bushes dressed as an usher and step on them before they can get back into the movie theater.

RICH TOSCHES

The article continues with a section called "Playing the Fish." Caution: If you confuse this with Playing the Violin, you're going to kill a lot of fish. And, of course, get a lot of strange looks when you try to hold the trout under your chin. This section of the actual article says you should set the hook if "the pod of fish scatters. One fish has felt the hook, spooks, and the others take the warning and run like a bunch of toddlers at bathtime."

I used this information just the other night when it was time to give my own toddler a bath. I can now report that I got him into the tub more quickly than ever before. On the downside, it took about forty minutes to get little Billy untangled from the net. And while I was toweling him off, he threw up a couple of caddis flies.

The article then says this (I swear I am not kidding):

> Often the trout will ignore the duns and focus on emergers as they struggle on the underside of the surface film, or meniscus. For tiny mayflies, breaking through the meniscus's rubbery barrier is akin to a human trying to dive through a swimming-pool cover.

The difference, generally, is that the trout is not drunk and isn't leaping off a motel balcony during spring-break week in North Dakota.

Anyway, armed with all of the knowledge gained from reading that *Fly Fisherman* article, I headed back up the mountain for the rematch. About an hour after I arrived, the surface feeding frenzy began, fish rising to my left, to my right, in front of me, and behind me. That last one surprised me because I was standing on the shore. As it turns out, it was a chipmunk—and a fierce one, too, as I found out while trying to unhook him.

But the point is, the feeding frenzy had begun, and this time I was ready. On my very first cast with a No. 22 emerger, a trout rose and sipped it off the surface, just like a whale, except quite a bit smaller.

I hooked another trout, a sixteen-inch cutthroat, about five minutes later and was feeling pretty darn good about myself. Then, as my fly lay motionless on the surface, a much larger fish approached, made a rush at the fly, and I yanked it away. Yanked in the sense that the fly, the leader, and about twenty feet of fly line came racing off the water and landed in an area that many leading fly casters would call "my face."

(The first time that happens to you, you scream and drop your fly rod. Fortunately, this was my 424th time, and I simply gathered up the line and continued casting a moment later, pausing occasionally to rub my face where the fly line had left welt marks, which are, as you might imagine, very painfulliness.)

During that marvelous day, I hooked and landed about a dozen dazzling trout. I missed about the same number of fish because, well, because let's just say it's hard to concentrate on fly-fishing when a chipmunk with a sore lip and a grudge is repeatedly attacking your ankle.

But I had, with the help of *Fly Fisherman* magazine, conquered the tough trout of North Mountain Lion Reservoir in Colorado. The only one who caught more fish than me on that lovely day was the guy fishing about fifty feet to my right. He must have caught a hundred! He said his name was Orville Redenbacher.

CHAPTER 12

My Eyes Adore Ewe

F act: The Arkansas River flows through Colorado.

Fact: The Colorado River does NOT flow through Arkansas.

This may seem somewhat unfair to the beautiful state of Arkansas. However, I would point out that life is not fair, and if the people of Arkansas feel cheated in any way, they may find some solace and comfort in the old Latin saying *Alestus wei non livum nei jirsei* ("At least we don't live in New Jersey").

Anyway, the Arkansas River is a marvelous eighty-mile stretch of trout water that gurgles from the

Rocky Mountains and flows through the old Spanish settlements of Buena Vista ("Ben is visiting") and Salida (town motto: "Don't Call Us Saliva"). It cuts through rugged canyons lined with cactus, yucca, and cows. You can differentiate between these three by patting them roughly on the head. The cactus and yucca will make you scream in pain, whereas the cows will moo.

As a bonus, several herds of Rocky Mountain bighorn sheep live in the canyons, and it is not unusual to see gatherings of male and female sheep as you fish the river. These sheep have even inspired many great songs, such as "My Eyes Adore Ewe" and "Ewe Are the Sunshine of My Life."

I am truly sorry for both of those stupid jokes, vow never again to stoop so low, and will now get on with a serious discussion about fishing the Arkansas River.

My introduction to this river came in the spring of 1995 when my good friend Karl Licis, who is a terrific outdoor writer for the *Colorado Springs Gazette,* invited me to accompany him for a day of fishing. The deal involved me doing all the driving, paying for all the gas, and buying lunch for him. In return, Karl would serve as the guide. Being a guide on this day turned out to be pretty easy, in the sense that once we got to the river, Karl pointed to a spot about a mile downstream and said, "Why don't you go way down there," and then vanished for the next five hours, leaving me, to use the old saying, holding my rod.

Fortunately, on this day I brought all of my extensive knowledge of entommol . . . entumology. . . . entamallog—bugs, and quickly matched the hatch. It helped that the air above the river was filled with what I would estimate to be 600 trillion jillion caddis flies. Further, after about an hour I noticed that when a caddis fly would ride on the surface of the water for even a few seconds, a trout would rise and pounce on it with a great big splash. (For the first fifty-five minutes I thought some asshole was throwing rocks into the water and I kept shouting for him to stop it.)

As I learned later, when it was getting dark and my good friend Karl dropped by and said he had to get home, it's known as the Mother's Day caddis hatch and happens every single year around Mother's Day, which I thought was pretty ironic.

Billions and billions of these insects hatch from the bottom of the river and make their way to the surface, where they dry their wings and then form huge flocks and fly south to their wintering grounds unless they are shot along the way, although I may be confusing the caddis fly with the Canada goose.

Here's all you need to know about fishing the caddis fly hatch on the Arkansas River: I caught—and I am not kidding about this—more than one hundred trout that day! I had not caught that many trout in the preceding thirty years of fly-fishing combined, unless you count that almost freakish incident in 1988 involving my cigarette lighter and that stick of dynamite on the famed Yellowstone River. (I netted one "whopper" that now hangs above my fireplace, and allowed the other eight hundred or so beautiful trout to drift back downstream, except for the few dozen that were up in the field and the one that went flying over the ranger's house.)

Seriously, I actually caught more than one hundred trout on the Arkansas River that day, most of them browns of thirteen to sixteen inches, all of them crashing the surface and gulping down a No. 16 elk-hair caddis. I had tied about thirty of these flies in preparation for the big day, which left me exhausted. Not so much from the actual tying of the flies, but from all the careful stalking through the Colorado mountains followed by all the running that

I was forced to do every time I yanked a clump of hair out of the elk's ass.

During one stretch, I caught fifteen trout in fifteen casts, all from a fifty-foot-long riffle, the fish rising savagely to the caddis. The presentation was very important. I found that I only caught a trout when I made a perfect cast, with the fly actually landing IN THE RIVER. (Although once, it landed about five feet up on the bank and a trout broke off an overhanging willow branch and began beating the fly with the branch, then dragged it back into the water. Okay, I made that part up.)

The casts were upstream, downstream, across the stream. It didn't make much difference. The trout sometimes hit it with even more vigor when it was being dragged across the surface by the current, a skittering move that imitated the natural movement of the struggling insects.

The fish gorge themselves outlandishly. Trout caught early in the morning are sleek and relatively thin. By the end of the day, almost all of the trout are fat, their stomachs swollen with food. If you can't make it to Colorado for this memorable few weeks of fishing, you can see pretty much the same thing in your own town—by following people for a few days after they walk proudly out of their last Weight Watchers class.

Since that unforgettable day with my friend Karl, I've brought many other friends to the caddis hatch on the Arkansas, beginners mostly, people who started the day with only the rudimentary skills of fly-fishing. By the end of the day, however, with me there to guide them, many of them were hooking branches and their own hats at nearly the same rate as "the master."

Mike Anton caught thirty-five trout during one day of the hatch in 1997. Prior to that day, his grand total of trout subdued

RICH TOSCHES

76

by a fly rod was zero. We packed away our rods in the evening and headed for the town of Saliva. Oops, I mean Salida, where we got a motel room and celebrated with fairly expensive beer and cigars, two men reveling in the thrill of fly-fishing and, more importantly, the fact that we'd found yet another way to get away from the house for a few days and behave like idiots.

We went to sleep after midnight, having depleted the supply of beer and cigars, and got back into the river the next morning with great eagerness, a burning sense of anticipation, and two unbelievable hangovers. At one point I started fishing deep with a nymph because the constant, loud *slap-slap-slap* of the trouts' tails on the surface felt as though it would make my head explode.

Mike was worse, though. He kept shouting "Jesus Christ, do they have to bang their wings on the water like that?" whenever a caddis fly tried to take off.

It was a bad day. We caught only forty or so trout between us. Which wasn't bad, considering I spent two hours on the bank, curled up under a bush, sleeping.

And that day I made an important decision about my health and my way of life: no more cigars!

So prodigious is the Mother's Day caddis-fly hatch on the Arkansas River that towns along the banks actually have celebrations. Most of these are sponsored by the chambers of commerce and celebrate the fact that fly fishermen tend to drop gigantic wads of cash wherever they go. The town of Canon City, for example, has a huge Caddis Fly Festival each spring, with music and dancing and booths selling T-shirts honoring the caddis fly.

Only one other fly in history has received so much attention.

That, of course, was President Bill Clinton's fly.

My fondest memory of caddis-fly-fishing, however, is the hatch of 2001. I brought my friend Susie, whom I'd introduced to the sport of fly-fishing just a few months earlier because of my feelings for her, my desire to see her enjoy nature as I do, and the mere pleasure of her company.

Okay, it was so I could go fly-fishing more often without having to beg.

Nevertheless, Susie took to fly-fishing like a duck to *l'orange* sauce. And it was during the caddis-fly hatch of 2001 that she became a devoted angler, catching and releasing nearly twenty brown trout in a day, and in just two days reaching a level of fly-fishing proficiency that took me more than ten years to attain.

This, she correctly pointed out, was because I'm an idiot.

Then she made me put out my cigar.

And made Mike get his own room.

In summary, the spring caddis hatch on the Arkansas River is nothing short of fantastic.

But just as the hatch and the feeding frenzy reach a peak, spring brings a wave of warm weather and the Rocky Mountain snows begin to melt. And quickly, the Arkansas River turns into a frightening, churning, dangerous body of rolling brown water, bringing with it the inevitable hordes of people in gigantic rafts, and for most anglers signaling the end of some of the most incredible fishing to be found anywhere.

Although I've found that some really wild action can continue well into the rafting season.

Especially if you make accurate casts, use about sixty-pound test tippet, and hook the rafters in that really sensitive area right under their nose.

CHAPTER 13

The Early Years, for Chrissakes

 I 'm thinking this might be a good time to tell you a little bit about the beginning of my fly-fishing life, sweeping you back to a time before my best friend made himself sick by eating a couple of cow faces, and before a World Fly-Fishing Championship entrant from Belgium looked me straight in the eye and said, in an excited way, "Mine fish dat small fish . . . neeeemph!"

It began, as I may or may not have pointed out at the start of the book, in Massachusetts. I grew up in the town of Hopedale in the southeast part of the

———

state. Hopedale had about three thousand residents and my public-high-school class had sixty-eight graduates. I was an excellent student and would have been the class valedictorian and also would have been officially ranked number one in my class if not for a technicality: about fifty-five of my classmates kept showing up at school (they were smarter than I).

So the teachers were left to tell my parents that I had "potential," which combines the French words *potent* ("powerful") and *ial* ("urge to screw around and disrupt class").

What none of them knew, however, is that by my twelfth birthday I had become possessed. Not in the satanic way. (Although once, in tenth grade, Vicki MacLean bent over to pick up some pencils while wearing a really short skirt and my head turned completely around—and the word *Yipes!* appeared on my stomach.)

No, I was possessed by fly-fishing. As I said a bit earlier, my father bought me my first fly rod that year—1967—and guided me through the early stages of my development as a fly fisherman. By this I mean every time he drove me to a nearby lake or stream, he'd shout, "For chrissakes be careful you're gonna close the car door on the damn rod and if it breaks so help me I am not getting you another one for chrissakes!"

I walked into the house one day and said: "I got a ride home, but Andy closed the car door on my fly rod and it broke."

Dad: "For chrissakes I told you . . . dammit to hell, dumb bastard closed the door on your fishing rod for chrissakes you shoulda been more careful! For Chrissakes!"

I told him I was just kidding and I think he laughed. Although it was hard to tell because he was breathing really hard as he chased me through the house swinging a mop handle. Later he calmed down and I heard him tell my mother, in a soft and gentle voice, "The kid's pretty fast. Dammit to hell, for chrissakes."

Anyway, my very first outing with my new fly rod was at nearby Louisa Lake, which was stocked with trout. As far as I could tell, perhaps two of them. Weeks went by without a single strike, as I clumsily tied knots and changed flies and untangled the fly line from around my head and my feet and tripped over my brand new hip boots. Eventually I got out of the car.

But finally, on a Saturday morning that in my mind seems as though it was yesterday (see Chapter 42: The Pot-Smoking Years), I caught my first trout. It was a rainbow, about twelve inches long, and it struck a wet fly that I'd been twitching along near the bottom of Louisa Lake. The strike was shocking to a young boy who had made hundreds and hundreds of casts without any response. Oh sure, I'd had plenty of firm tugs on the line during previous outings, but this one was different. Mostly because there wasn't any blood coming from my ear and I wasn't crying "Someone, please, get the hook out of my ear, for chrissakes!" as I'd done so many times in the past.

No, by golly, this was a trout and my heart raced with excitement. It struggled valiantly, but I soon landed him, using a technique I still enjoy today that involves stumbling backward and dragging the fish about fifteen feet up onto the shore, then dropping the rod and sprinting toward the fish while yelling "Got one!"

I let that trout go on that sparkling day, as I've done with virtually all trout I've caught in the many decades since. Catch-and-release, I feel, is the most critical aspect of this sport, a gentle nod by the angler to our Creator as we say, "Thank You for giving us such special creatures and the magnificence of the natural world they live in, but now, God, I shall return it to battle yet another day with another angler."

And, of course, because trout taste like fish, and frankly, I'd rather eat a sweatsock.

Anyway, I released my first trout, watching in wonder as he swam back out into the lake, where I'm guessing he took quite a ribbing from his friends. ("You were caught by WHO?") And then I sat on the shore, breathless, realizing at the age of twelve that I'd found something magical.

My next great experience in fly-fishing came about a month later, at a nearby pond at the Nipmuc Rod and Gun Club, of which I was a junior member. And, without sounding as though I'm bragging, I was probably the most amazing junior member the rod and gun club ever had. I've been told that old men still gather at the skeet range and talk in hushed tones of the day the spring-loaded launcher broke and they gave a kid $2 to run across the range, holding clay pigeons over his head.

Anyway, the Nipmuc pond held a lot more trout than Louisa Lake, and one day, after my father had dropped me off near the shore and wished me well ("Don't fall in, for chrissakes!") I saw something that made my heart thump: a large trout rising to the surface for insects. I didn't even know trout did that!

I had about five or six dry flies that I kept in a plastic film canister, and picked out one that looked like a moth. After a long struggle to tie it to the leader—in those early days, tying knots often involved all ten fingers, a couple of toes, and a stick—I began my approach. The fish was rising steadily near the dam, a concrete structure that rose about four feet off the ground. I scrambled onto the dam and began making beautiful, graceful twenty-foot casts out onto the lake, which was terrific for a kid my age. Unfortunately, the fish was rising about forty feet out onto the lake. Suddenly, however, the fish moved closer. *Splash.* He rose within casting distance and I set the giant moth down about five feet from him.

I remember everything being blurry. A fluffy cloud went by. I was no longer looking at the trout or even at the pond. I was looking straight up. And having a great amount of difficulty—to use the formal fly-fishing term—"breathing." From the account given to me by my friend Kevin Smith, who was about twenty feet away at the time, here's what happened:

My giant moth had just settled onto the water when *bang*—the big trout struck. I vaguely recall seeing that. I'm told I reacted by pulling quite forcefully on the line and the rod, along with making a frighteningly loud sound like Yaaaaaeeeeeooohhhhhhh!

Then I fell off the dam. Backward. Onto my back. Needless to say, I didn't hook the trout.

Today, after thousands and thousands of hours in some of the most breathtaking places on earth in search of the elusive trout, I know that when a big trout crashes a dry fly like that, you have to be patient, waiting one or two seconds for him to engulf the fly and turn back down with it firmly in his mouth.

Then, and only then, do you lift the rod, smiling with that great feeling of accomplishment as the fly comes out of his mouth and you fall backward off the dam.

CHAPTER 14

My First Giant Rubber Pants

I'd fly-fished the lakes and ponds around my home for about two years before venturing into moving water. The debut of my creek-fishing skills came in Muddy Brook, a meandering stream that went through our town and neighboring villages, often cutting across cow pastures. I'd stare at the flowing water and wonder what array of insects the trout were feeding on and how I'd drift a fly down into the pools where they lurked. My friend Rob, who also grew up in Hopedale, would usually lag behind on these outings, staring at the cows and wondering how their cheek meat would taste rolled up in a flour tortilla.

Transportation on these adventures generally consisted of bicycles, the cool ones with the banana seats and the really high handlebars. As I'd set off on my journeys, holding my fly rod across the handlebars and clutching a sack of flies and spools of monofilament line that would serve as leader, my father would stand on the porch, watching his little boy growing up, and offer words of encouragement.

"For chrissakes, you're gonna fall off and break your neck!" would be one example.

This would usually be followed by: "And don't get that rod stuck in the spokes or you'll break the goddamn thing. For chrissakes!"

I'd pedal furiously to my destination, often a pasture in the nearby town of Mendon, where Muddy Brook grew deep and wide and fifteen-inch trout lurked behind the rocks. Sometimes I'd spend half an hour just watching, sitting in the grass, hoping the cows would not move any closer. I was afraid of cows back then. Of course I was just a kid. Now, at the age of forty-six, I am also afraid of goats and sheep.

Anyway, I'd sit in the grass in the early morning and wait until the air warmed and a few insects would appear. They were mayflies, I think, and as the sun rose higher they would come in small clouds from the water, followed by the trout. I'd spend hour after hour drifting tiny flies into the pools but never, ever caught a trout off the surface in those early years. I'm guessing the leader was too heavy and perhaps the fly dragged across the surface. But later, when the surface activity would stop, well, that's when I'd catch trout. A small nymph drifted deep would do the trick, the leader giving a telltale twitch at the strike.

I'd caught three or four small trout one day, the largest being about thirteen inches, when suddenly the leader darted violently to the right and I set the hook on Moby Trout. My heart raced as the fish roared downstream, the fly line tearing through my hands as I ran alongside, sometimes stepping in "meadow muffins" the cows had left along the stream.

When I was done fishing on those days I'd meet up with my friends, who had usually spent the day playing baseball or basketball. They knew where I'd been, my reputation as a fly fisherman having spread from one end of town to the other, a distance of exactly three miles. They'd look at me on those quiet summer evenings and I'd sense a bit of envy in their eyes, knowing I had stepped beyond the normal boundaries of youth and was, day by day, teaching myself the art of fly-fishing. Sometimes, this jealousy would show itself in their quiet whispers as I approached. An example would be: "Here comes Tosches. I bet he's got cow shit on his shoes again."

Back at Muddy Brook, the huge trout had taken me about two hundred feet downstream before I could turn him, adrenaline racing through my veins as I gently brought him toward me. And then, standing knee-deep in the water in my blue jeans, I slid him onto a sandbar near the shore and let out a shout of glee, a boy crying out in sheer joy at the wonder of it all. Although to the cows, it may have sounded like "Shit! It's a carp!"

It was a lovely carp, though, perhaps eight pounds of puckered lips, beady eyes, swollen stomach, and slimy scales. And I'm not sure why, but some thirty years later the memory of that moment came racing back to me.

I think it was the day I met Jeffrey, my ex-wife's divorce attorney.

Muddy Brook wasn't my only special place, though. Another

was the West River, which required about a five-mile bike ride, uphill. Both ways.

The West River was a classic tail water fishery, although that term had not yet been invented and I just called it "fishing under the dam." By then I had my first pair of waders, allowing me to get into the right position to make my casts and probe all parts of the nearby streams and river, opening up a whole new aspect of fly-fishing. And the whispers of my friends changed, too. ("Here comes Tosches. I bet he's wearing those giant rubber pants again.")

But these giant rubber pants put me in position to make long drifts with a nymph along the bottom of the West River where the water emerged from the dam, and this, I'd found, was where the trout waited for their food. I didn't know about nymph indicators back then, which now consist of polymer yarns and fluorescent cork and dozens of other high-tech tools that allow you to detect the most subtle strike. I used—I'm not kidding—pieces of wood carved from the branches of nearby trees, held to the fly line with thread. It worked just fine. And when you've got a three-inch piece of rough wood whistling by your face all day, well, it taught me a lot about concentration and proper casting techniques.

And, of course, it taught me a lot about ducking.

But I caught trout this way, and that's all that mattered. The small, floating piece of wood would twitch or pause in the current and I'd set the hook and feel the gentle tug of a trout, and at that moment, to a young boy alone on a trout stream, the world was a magical place. I say "magical" because for about five years, my time-consuming obsession with fly-fishing somehow caused my schoolwork to vanish. Although amazingly, I was still able, once in a while, to pull some decent grades out of my a . . . uh, out of my *sleeve*.

RICH TOSCHES

CHAPTER 15

Alpha Chi Cheese

I left Massachusetts in 1973, bound for Marquette University in Milwaukee, Wisconsin, a nice city tucked against the shore of Lake Michigan. I brought my fly rod, of course, and it didn't take me long to figure out what I'd be doing for the next four years. That's right: drinking beer.

Once in a while, though, I'd step over the cases of empty Red White and Blue brand beer bottles that littered the house I shared with seven other guys, and I'd head past the campus and down to the lakefront, where the people of Milwaukee would gather with friends and family to breathe the fresh air and marvel at the expanse of water stretching to the horizon.

Okay, they were all at the lake's shore drinking beer and throwing up cheese.

But the point is, I would often board a city bus for the thirty-block ride to Lake Michigan to throw a fly into the deep, clear water. The first few trips were disappointing. I'd occasionally see a fish rise to the surface, but they showed no interest in the dry flies I offered. The shoreline in the fall and again in the spring was patrolled by big brown trout, I was told, so I eventually switched to a sinking line with big streamers and woolly buggers and began getting thumped by monstrous trout.

And nearly flunked out of college.

By the midsemester mark of my freshman year, I'd been summoned to the office of the dean of the journalism college and shown my grades. I had a C-minus in an English class, D's in civics and science, and an F in a math class.

As much as I loved fly-fishing, it was obvious that something was wrong with the way I was allocating my time.

Clearly, I was spending too much time on the English class.

So I vowed to make some adjustments and begged the assistant dean not to send these midsemester grade reports to my parents. They were spending about $10,000 a year to send me to this fine school and I didn't want them to worry needlessly. And, of course, I was having enough problems without the thought of my angry father jumping into his 1970 Mercury and driving a thousand miles to Wisconsin while mumbling "I'll give the little bastard some fly-fishing goddammit to hell wasting my damn money for chrissakes!"

Which would, I believed, be followed by me spending weeks of valuable study time trying to get a nine-foot, six-weight Shakespeare fly rod out of my ass.

So I tucked the fly rod away for a while and brought the grades up to a respectable level.

I slept through most of the winter, when temperatures would drop to thirty degrees (Fahrenheit) below zero, which was either 1,566 degrees Celsius or six cubic hectares. (My struggle with science continued.)

But then spring came to this lovely land, and the people celebrated by rubbing their noses together in greeting and dancing around the seal carcasses. I celebrated by taking out the fly rod and heading to the lake. On that first outing of the year, in April of 1974, I hooked six huge browns on a streamer fly, the wild fish tearing fly line and backing from the reel until I would eventually work them up onto the beach. People would gather around during the battles, swearing excitedly in a way that made me homesick.

And then, when I'd release the huge trout, they'd ask the question I'd been hearing since I began fishing:

"Aren't ya gonna eat them?"

No, I'd say to these fine, God-fearing people of Wisconsin, I was not going to eat the fish. I'd try to explain the catch-and-release concept—conserving valuable resources, the joy I felt in watching a fish return to its habitat—and would then make the explanation understandable by comparing a wild brown trout to cheese.

Cheese, they'd nod in agreement, is seldom released.

The exception to that rule involved my roommate, George McCullough, a big, lovable farm boy from Chesterfield, Missouri, who would often "release the cheese." Always in the middle of the night, when we were locked in our airtight dormitory room.

(I'm just kidding, of course. Sometimes George would release the cheese during a class. Or during a date.)

In four years of fly-fishing the shoreline of Lake Michigan, I only kept two trout. Let me tell you the story.

On my twenty-first birthday, my buddies took me out to celebrate. We laughed and drank beer and then they shoved my head into a disgustingly filthy public men's-room toilet in the Avalanche Bar, which was a big hangout for homeless people, and flushed it. This was called a "swirly" and was meant to convey their affection. What it actually did was force me to stagger back to our house and wash my hair nonstop for two hours, with dish soap. When I finally emerged from the shower, I'm proud to say that my hair contained only a very faint aroma of a homeless guy's ass.

I don't want to get into a long-drawn-out discussion of the word *revenge,* so let me get to the point. A week later I caught a pair of twenty-two-inch brown trout. I kept them. We cooked them that night and my dear old pals thanked me for the fine meal.

Three nights later Jim "Wild Bull" Bristol returned home around midnight. Jim, or JB, is a big, rugged, manly man who scared us. Anyway, he went into his very dark room that night, reached for the light chain dangling from the socket over his bed—and grabbed a handful of brown trout head that had somehow tied itself to the chain.

Today, some twenty-four years later, I can still hear the sissylike sound of "eeeeeeeeeeee!!!!!" that came out of JB's room that night. When he emerged a moment later his testosterone level had returned to normal and he strutted around for a while ("I saw it. I didn't touch it!") before slipping into the bathroom to wash his hands with bleach.

———

RICH TOSCHES

And we were all still laughing about it the next morning, when suddenly, the voice of Tom Murphy—I think he had been holding my feet when my head went into the toilet—echoed from upstairs: "Jesus Christ! There's a #$%^!@# fish head in my $%^&*(@ underwear!"

I told him that was disgusting, and he might want to start changing his shorts a bit more frequently.

I miss my college buddies.

The bastards.

CHAPTER 16

Vince Lombardi Didn't Fly-Fish

I n the spring of 1977, with my degree in journalism all but assured thanks to four years of diligent study—and, according to my doctor, with nearly 15 percent of my liver still functioning—I took a three-day weekend, which was quite unusual. Most of my weekends in college were five or six days.

Anyway, needing a break from all the hard work, I packed up my fly-fishing gear and boarded a Greyhound bus, heading for the wilds of northern Wisconsin. The bus stopped in lovely towns such as Sheboygan (a Native American word meaning "the chief is dressing up in women's clothes again") and Manitowoc ("screw Manny, let's make him walk") and on into the famous town of Green Bay—where legendary Packers football coach Vince Lombardi would often stand and, in a voice choked with emotion and filled with the love he had for his players, say proudly, "How the hell did I end up here?"

After about a twenty-minute stop at the Greyhound station, which gave the passenger sitting next to me time to grab a cup of coffee before returning to his seat and resuming talking to himself, we were off again. Soon we'd reached my destination: the tiny town of Fish Creek on the sixty-mile-long peninsula separating Lake Michigan from the waters of Green Bay. I got a decent motel room for $19 a night—today, of course, the same room goes for $21.99 a night—and began hiking the trails of Peninsula State Park with my fly rod.

What I saw remains forever etched in my mind: gigantic chinook salmon, cruising the deep, clear waters along the shoreline at the mouths of tiny creeks. Concealing myself in shrubs along the creek banks, I could creep within a couple of feet and watch the fish, some I estimated at fifteen and twenty pounds, shoot past me in three and four feet of water. It was breathtaking. Soon I was actually in the creek, plunging my head into the icy water and emerging with a huge, thrashing salmon in my mouth, part of which I ate myself and part I gave to my young cubs, although I may be confusing my own personal experience in the Wisconsin north country twenty-four years ago with a Discovery Channel special I watched last night.

Have I mentioned that my friends and I drank a lot of beer during the college days?

My attempts to catch one of these monster salmon was a real

hoot. For a few hours I cast a bright orange streamer into the bay, where I could see the fish cruising, waiting for that biological trigger that sends them up the stream, according to wildlife biologists, like Bill Clinton heading for the Oval Office rest room. Only once did a salmon show any interest in the gaudy streamer, following it nearly to the shore before turning away. I recall making loud shouting noises and having to sit down because my knees were weak.

So I moved one hundred feet up the stream, switched to a small egg pattern, and waited. You could see the salmon come over a gravel bar and then into the pool where I crouched. After a dozen or so casts, a huge salmon nailed the egg and headed upstream, with me sprinting behind. I ran through the bushes and I ran through the brambles. I ran through the briars where a rabbit couldn't go—which I predict will someday become lyrics to a hillbilly country song.

The stream was no more than ten feet wide, and the salmon cut straight up the middle, tearing into my backing as I stumbled through the shrubs. I have never—before or since—felt such an indescribable rush of pure excitement, which tells you a lot about fly-fishing and, perhaps, why I've been married and divorced twice.

I never caught that giant salmon. He just kept going. Eventually, with thirty yards of fly line and perhaps twenty more yards of backing separating us, the line simply went slack and began drifting back downstream. I reeled it in and sat, shaking, in the lush green forest.

In the Adam Sandler movie *Happy Gilmore*—which is considered a film classic by not just me but many, many other idiots—Happy's golf instructor teaches him to relax by remembering a good time in his life, or as it is called, "going to his happy place."

Fly-fishing has given me a dozen or more happy places, sun-dappled streams or glistening lakes that are so firmly burned into the memory that I can still smell the wildflowers in a New Zealand meadow, still see the trout rising to my dry fly on my hometown trout pond when I was just a kid. And I can still feel the heart-pounding thrill of that wonderful spring day in Wisconsin when a monstrous salmon left me dazed and breathless.

The bastard.

CHAPTER 17

Goin' Hollywood

In 1977 I found myself getting off an airplane in Los Angeles, where I would live for the next fifteen years, first as a reporter for United Press International and then for the *Los Angeles Times*. Los Angeles offers a lot of things. I had lunch with Bob Hope, for example. Just Bob and I, dining on pork chops and talking about college football, sitting at the table in his Toluca Lake neighborhood home, which had a three-hole golf course in the backyard. By way of comparison, my backyard had an assortment of homeless people who would occasionally charge at me before toppling into the shrubs and peeing in their pants. Bob Hope's house was a lot nicer.

I covered earthquakes and raging wildfires and once, about six weeks into my career, answered the phone in the L.A. bureau of the UPI wire service and the man on the other end said, "Hi. This is John Wayne."

It sounded sorta like the great actor, too, but I was busy writing the regional weather summary for the day, and as we got perhaps a hundred calls from loons each day, I replied, "Right. And I'm Roy Rogers." And I hung up.

Five minutes later the bureau manager, John Lowry, emerged from his office with a gigantic vein protruding on his forehead. "YOU JUST HUNG UP ON JOHN WAYNE, YOU STUPID SON OF A BITCH!" he said. Back then it was okay to talk to your employees that way. Today, of course, with labor lawyers and political correctness and workplace sensitivity, a thing like that would never happen because, well, mostly because John Wayne is dead.

I also covered three Super Bowls. After one, Dan Marino of the Miami Dolphins removed white athletic tape from his ankles, balled it up, and after I kicked off the locker-room interview session by throwing out the ceremonial first stupid question, Dan threw the ball of tape at me and hit me in the eye. I'm not kidding. He then apologized and said I could ask another question. I went with "If you were a tree, what kind of tree would you be?" The great quarterback came at me with scissors.

I also covered three World Series, highlighted by the 1981 series between the Los Angeles Dodgers and the New York Yankees in which Reggie Jackson called me an asshole and walked away from an interview. And I hadn't even gotten to the question about the tree.

The most memorable moment of my baseball-writing days, however, came in the Dodgers locker room after a game in the early 1980s when Dodger outfielder Pedro Guerrero, who was from the Dominican Republic, walked past manager Tommy Lasorda's office, which was filled with about a dozen writers. Pedro was naked. Seeing his star slugger, manager Lasorda—and I swear to God I am not making this up—shouted, "Hey, Pete! Come on in here and tell these guys about that time in Mexico when you f#%^&*# that goat!"

Guerrero, standing naked in the doorway, laughed and replied, "Oh, 'Sorda, that was a long time ago!" and walked away, scratching his ass.

Yup, I've been to the mountaintop!

Oh, and I also covered boxing for three years. For an in-depth study of the brutal sport I climbed into the ring, in 1987, with then world middleweight champion Michael Nunn. He beat me senseless for three rounds, leaving my eyes swollen, my lips swollen, and my nose swollen. When it was over he came to my corner and asked if I was okay, to which I replied, "Ghafgth ba-hagamoof, thampghs."

Did I mention that my lips were swollen?

All in all, it was a hoot.

What Los Angeles didn't offer, however, was much in the way of fly-fishing. Everything was more or less paved. The exception, of course, was the ocean, which the city of Los Angeles could not pave because, as I understand it, Johnny Carson owns it. But we could still use it, and within a few months of my arrival I found myself standing at the harbor in the nearby town of Redondo Beach. The surface of the water was being churned white as fast-moving fish slashed through schools of baitfish no more than twenty feet from the rock jetty I was standing on. My fly-fishing instinct kicked in and I did exactly what you'd figure a guy would do in that situation. That's right, I stared at the blonde with the roller skates and the gargantuan fake breasts until drool covered the entire front of my shirt.

About a week later I went back to the Redondo harbor, this time armed with my fly rod and an assortment of saltwater streamer flies I'd picked up at a tackle shop. The fish, I was told, were bonito. What I was not told was that bonito are like trout on steroids, and trying to stop one with a six-weight fly rod is not easy. Especially when the reel you own has an intricate drag system that basically consists of the handle smashing into your fingers as it goes around at about 4,500 rpm and you shouting "Holy shit!" over and over again.

I got into position on the rock jetty. The water was still. About twenty minutes later, however, I saw the bonito crashing the surface and moving in my direction. A long cast dropped a white streamer into the middle of the frenzy and then I just hung on as a fish struck and—despite my repeated cries of "Holy shit!"—headed straight out into the Pacific Ocean toward Holland or Wales or whatever's on the other side of the Pacific Ocean. (I wasn't very good in geometry.)

Somehow, though, the bonito eventually turned and I wrestled it back toward the rocks, sliding it into a space between two boulders and unhooking it. At which point it slammed its powerful tail against my hand, which in turn crashed into a rock. It hurt so much I staggered backward and fell on the slick, seaweed-covered rocks, banging my right hip on a jagged boulder. So there I lay, my hand bleeding, my ass going numb, twisted into a tiny pathetic little heap on rocks covered with seagull poop.

I was the happiest guy in the world.

You know, if you don't count Richard Simmons.

In this strange new land that I would call home for a decade and a half, I had found my little place, my happy place, a place that would sweep me away from the mad life I was living just a few miles inland, a place called Redondo Beach—home to seals and sea lions and blondes with huge artificial breasts and, of course, bonito, which had regular, normal breasts. I think.

CHAPTER 18

Maggie Meets Mr. High Jumpy Guy

Eventually, though, the lure of the wily trout had me exploring streams around Los Angeles. There were very few places. One was called Piru Creek, about fifty miles to the north, although Piru lost some of its appeal for me when seven Vietnamese refugees—I am not kidding—were arrested for blowing up trout in the stream with sticks of dynamite and netting the fish as they floated downstream. The men seemed quite puzzled by the whole legal mess, scratching their heads during a court appearance and saying over and over again, in sad, plaintive voices,

"Tam won hangue guanade" ("Next time we'll use hand grenades like everyone else").

My quest for trout fishing eventually brought me to the Sierras, a stunning chain of mountains that runs through Yosemite National Park about a five-hour drive north of L.A.—unless gang members believe you have cut them off in traffic on the Hollywood Freeway and begin chasing you, which allows you to cover the 275 miles in fifty minutes. (Gang members don't seem real interested in fly-fishing, despite the obvious connection: a pair of extra-large breathable Orvis waders look exactly like the gigantic trousers they enjoy wearing, pants apparently stolen from their grandfathers.)

An early discovery for me was the Kern River, which held a fair number of browns and rainbows. On my first outing along this river, I watched a grasshopper fall from the streamside brush and immediately disappear into the swirl of a good-sized fish. I quickly tied on a hopper imitation and, well, I don't think I have to tell you veteran fly anglers what happened next. That's right, my first cast caught the bush on the opposite bank and I snapped the leader trying to get the grasshopper out. Unfortunately, it was my only grasshopper, so I spent the next two hours using a lot of foul language as I went through about two dozen other flies in my box without a strike.

Then, perhaps out of frustration, perhaps because I'm an idiot with few principles, I caught a live grasshopper, pinned him to the hook of a No. 10 Adams, which looked like a moth, and tossed the whole mess out into the middle of the Kern River.

A brown trout came to this odd combination in a hurry. I don't know why, although my extensive knowledge of entomology tells me that the trout believed the giant moth was going to carry the grasshopper off, and dammit, he was going to get a bite of *something* before the buffet table flew away.

The trout was released unharmed, and I suddenly felt terribly guilty about having resorted to the use of live bait. This nagging guilt haunted me for the rest of the day, hanging on to me like a heavy weight that, I believe, slowed me down as I raced around in the grass and threw myself onto more grasshoppers, trying not to let the little bastards bite me as I stuffed them into a vest pocket and went sprinting back toward the river.

I'm just kidding, of course. I sent my daughter, Maggie, who was three, after the grasshoppers.

Maggie held a small cardboard box as she lurched around in the tall grass, a squeal of delight echoing through the valley with each capture. When she'd bring the 'hopper to me, I'd say things such as "We'll name this one Mr. High Jumpy Guy and he can be our new pet." Then she'd return to the grass fifty feet away and I'd have Mr. High Jumpy Guy drifting down the middle of the Kern River, attached to his new friend, Mr. Moth.

When Maggie returned with another grasshopper, I told her the first one had jumped back into the grass, probably to be with his family, whom he loved very much, and we'd keep this *new* grasshopper as a pet and name him Mr. Leap High Into The Air Guy. He, too, would later "escape"—as would each and every one of the dozen or more grasshoppers little Maggie brought to her daddy that day.

Today, I've matured a lot and promise that I will never, ever again do anything so despicable. These days I pursue the trout fairly, using only the artificial flies that I keep on my fly-fishing vest, on that little patch of wool that hangs over the left pocket.

Just above the hand grenade.

———

ZIPPING MY FLY

CHAPTER 19

Oh No! Not the Cows!

After a few years in L.A. it occurred to me that to do any real fly fishing I'd have to get on a plane. Luckily, my boyhood friend Rob had settled in Boulder, Colorado, and had mistakenly given me his phone number and address.

In the early 1980s I began making annual journeys with Rob and other friends through Colorado ("The Lone Star State") and neighboring Wyoming ("I Swear I Was Just Helping the Sheep Through the Fence!"). We called these events "elk-hunting trips" and would usually go as far as to purchase an elk license and actually bring rifles along. In twelve years of these alleged hunting trips, the closest I actually came to an elk was in 1984—when a gust of wind along the North Platte River in Wyoming caused a No. 16 elk-hair caddis to become embedded in my right earlobe. As you might imagine, this was unbelievably painful and I spent the better part of the afternoon screaming and falling into the grassy field along the river, trying to pull the fly out of my ear.

Back at the cabin that night, Rob and I swapped tales of our day in the great outdoors. I told him about having the elk-hair caddis in my ear, but he topped that one. Apparently he had an elk in his crosshairs several times during his hunt—but claimed that every time he was about to pull the trigger, the elk would disappear into the tall grass.

And he'd hear a man scream.

The destination during those years was the Wyoming town of Saratoga in the Medicine Bow National Forest. I'd fly from Los Angeles to Denver, and often the trip from the Denver airport to Wyoming was the highlight of the journey. In 1980, for example, the three-hour drive in Rob's small Toyota pickup took place during a pounding rain-and-sleet storm, with passing vehicles throwing up a relentless spray of brown water and mud from the road. Rob had prepared for just such an event by draining the windshield-washer-fluid reservoir in his truck and disconnecting the hose. That trip was a lot of fun.

As a bonus, I now know the thrill Stevie Wonder must get when he gets a sudden rush of independence, sneaks past the servants, fires up the Mercedes, and heads down to Burger King.

Another memorable trip from Denver to Wyoming came in 1982, when Rob's International Scout blew both headlights on the last leg of the trip, which was down the side of a mountain in the Medicine Bow range. At midnight.

This—I'm not kidding—is how we navigated the final eight miles of that trip: me sitting on the hood of the truck, shining a flashlight on the roadway, trying to dig my fingernails into the paint to keep from sliding off as Rob sent the truck hurtling downhill at 50 mph. It was fifteen degrees at the time, and using the National Weather Service conversion chart, I can tell you that on that night some twenty years ago, the combination of the temperature and the man-made 50-mph wind created a windchill factor somewhere between "Pretty Damn Cold" and "To This Day I Still Have Not Gotten Much Feeling Back in My Testicles."

But that was a long time ago and I've forgiven Rob and no longer dwell on the incident.

And the presence of the North Platte River made the epic struggles worthwhile. One of the last great freestone rivers in the West, the North Platte meanders through lush forests and meadows, with as many as five thousand wild trout per mile, most of them smart enough to (a) Never hold a flashlight and sit on the hood of a fast-moving truck being driven by an idiot; and (b) Keep their testicles safely tucked away inside their warm body so, in the event they ever needed them, they could ACTU-ALLY USE THEM!

Sorry.

I will now tell just four stories culled from hundreds of interesting moments during a long love affair with the area around Saratoga, Wyoming, and the North Platte River. (I would tell more, but all the other stories involve whiskey, livestock, and women's clothing and would be horribly embarrassing to Rob, who is now the chief probation officer for Boulder County.)

The Nice People on the Deck

I met the nice people on the deck in 1988. I had hiked about four miles from a parking area along the North Platte, fighting my way through bushes and briars, fishing each likely hole, and catching a few nice trout. Then, through the forest, I saw a cabin. It was built on the river. And the deck actually hung over the river.

Here I will cite Wyoming law, specifically Chapter 43, Subsection IV, Paragraph 14: "If a resident of a rural region of the state attends a 'moving picture show' prior to 4 P.M. on days designated as *weekdays,* said resident shall be admitted for $2, and the sheep shall be admitted free."

Oops. Wrong law.

The one I'm talking about deals with ownership of river property. It says that a landowner may own half of the river. In other words, if you drew a line down the middle of the Platte River, well, your pen would get wet and you'd probably drown, you damn fool!

No, what it means is that if you drew an *imaginary* line down the middle of the river, the landowner owns the half bordering his land and no one may step upon the bottom of the river on the landowner's side!

Which is one of the reasons you seldom hear the expression "good ol' Wyoming wisdom."

You can, however, fish on the landowner's side by making long casts. Which brings us back to the nice people on the deck. As I approached the cabin and the lovely, swirling pool of trout in front of it, I was welcomed by a hand-painted sign hanging from the deck. The actual sign read:

YOU'VE GOT THE WHOLE RIVER TO FISH IN. DON'T FISH HERE!

———

RICH TOSCHES

As I understand it, the cabin's owners went with that particular wording because they didn't have enough paint for:

HEY DICKHEAD! WHY DON'T YOU STICK THAT FLY ROD UP YOUR ASS? OR WAIT, I KNOW . . . MAYBE WE COULD JUST SHOOT YOU! WE HATE EVERYBODY! WE WERE DROPPED ON OUR HEADS AS BABIES AND FRANKLY, WE'RE THE ONLY TWO PEOPLE ON EARTH WHO CAN STAND EACH OTHER. (AND JUST BETWEEN US, ABOUT TWICE A WEEK I EVEN THINK ABOUT THROWING *HER* INTO THE GODDAMN RIVER!) YOU BASTARDS!!!

Anyway, I did what anyone would do when confronted with such a message, telling me, in no uncertain terms, that I was not wanted. That's right; I switched to a No. 16 blue-winged olive, stripped out about forty feet of line, and started nailing some huge rainbows in a nice little seam against the opposite bank.

This brought the nice people onto their deck. Even though I was fishing legally, from the other side of the river, the woman began screaming at me. She called me a son of a bitch, a term I had not heard since, well, since about eight that morning when I grabbed my sack lunch—and my friend Rob's—off the front seat of his truck and sprinted into the woods.

The man rolled out onto the deck in a wheelchair and I immediately felt sorry for him. Not because he was in a wheelchair but because he was trapped, probably for the rest of his life, in a small cabin with this bitch. I figured not being able to walk probably wasn't even on his top-ten list of Things That Make Life Unpleasant.

I told the woman, in a calm voice, that I was fishing legally. That Wyoming law allowed me to make casts from the opposite side of the river. That the fish in the entire river belonged to the state of Wyoming. That there was currently a fine hatch of blue-winged olives under way, and that I would release all of the trout unharmed and would not make a peep or leave so much as a gum wrapper as I fished for the next thirty minutes or so before heading upstream.

"Get out of here now, you son of a bitch!" she screamed.

At that moment a huge rainbow rose to my fly, gulped it in, and the battle was on. It stripped line from my reel on this fine October day, slashing through the two-hundred-yard-long pool nearly beneath the feet of Cuckoo Woman as I stayed firmly planted on my side of the river. Eventually the trout—twenty-four inches of trout—came to my net beneath a towering cotton-wood tree of yellow leaves.

And I realized that for those five minutes I'd been immersed so deeply in my own world, a magnificent world of fly-fishing and giant trout on a wild river in Wyoming, that I had blocked out the unpleasantness that was attacking my ears and now had only a vague recollection of a babbling, nagging woman hovering over me and screaming at me.

And I had this thought: "If fly-fishing isn't good training for being a husband, what is?"

The Cows Are Trying to Drown Me

It was on a warm October day in 1979 that I found a stretch of the North Platte River that was bordered by farmland, the flowing water sparkling in the autumn sun, the kind of water that seems to be begging to be fly-fished by a moron. Recalling bumper stickers I had seen, I had my kid beat up your honor-student kid. Oops. Wrong bumper sticker. The one I mean says ASK FIRST!—and so I tracked down the landowner and asked permission to fish on his property.

He gave his approval and then added these words: "Be careful of the cows."

Be careful of the cows?

First of all, I couldn't see any cows. I had seen two white-tailed deer off the in distance as I walked along a road near his ranch-land, and I wondered now if the amiable fellow thought they were cows. This is what can happen to you when you spend endless hours sitting on a horse in the hot sun, worrying about all the things ranchers worry about—mostly why your three sons insist on living in your house despite the fact that they are in their forties, and one of them calls himself "Hoss" and eats so goddamn much that your cook, Hop Sing, has tried to poison him, and the fact they never seem to have any girlfriends, which makes you wonder if maybe all three of them are gay!

Sorry.

Second, I wondered just how careful you have to be with cows when you're armed with nothing more than a five-weight St. Croix fly rod and a boxful of dry flies? I mean, even if you accidentally hook one, I'm sure the 6X tippet would break before the cow got into your backing—unless you were using Rio-brand leader material with superb abrasion resistance plus high knot and tensile strength.

I bet that will get me a big fat sponsor contract! I can see the new advertisement series now, featuring me saying: "Use Rio leaders and tippet. It can stop a cow!"

Anyway, I thanked the man and headed downstream and found a spectacular looking pool at the tail of some riffles. I sat on the bank for a few moments and saw heads popping up, heads of big rainbows slurping Tricos. I tied on my favorite, a parachute Trico, which is like a regular Trico except just as it hits the water a man leaps from an airplane, pulls the rip cord, and lands safely on the tiny fly.

No, a parachute has a tuft of hair that you can actually see from more than twelve inches away, making it the ideal fly for those few people who cannot see a fly the size of a pinhead floating thirty feet away with the sun in their eyes—the losers.

On my fifth or sixth cast, the fly made a nice drag-free float and a trout sucked it in and we battled then under the warm fall sun, a sixteen-inch rainbow eventually sliding onto a gravel bar at my feet. I released the fish and caught four more in the next half hour, a thrill that made me lean my head back, gaze at the deep blue sky, and say out loud, "Mooooo!"

Turns out that wasn't me. It was a cow that had, along with perhaps twenty-five of her friends, snuck up behind me in that stealthy, leopardlike way that cows have. I turned and admired the cows—huge creatures with brown hair covering their entire bodies, enormously large asses, and big eyes and eyelashes—and I thought, "I wonder what my high-school prom date is doing these days?"

The cows kept inching closer to the river, looking—and here I use the old expression—"thirsty as cows." I moved a few feet downstream, but three of the cows moved, too, and cut me off. Then a few stepped down off the upstream bank and held their ground as the main attack force of cows lurched off the bank toward me.

There comes a time in a man's life when he's forced to ponder the meaning of life. This generally comes after about eight beers, and sometime around midnight we settle on this: "Thank the Good Lord Jesus Christ that that I am not married to Martha Stewart!"

———

I had not had any beers on this fine day in the wild lands of Wyoming, but I pondered the meaning of life anyway and came up with this: I am about to die a bizarre death that will involve cows, a fly rod, and a lot of swearing.

The cows kept coming now, coming in waves off the grassy bank. They had no fear of humans, particularly of one who was shouting "Bad cows! Get away! Shooooo, goddammit!"

I even tried yelling "How now, brown cow?" but that didn't work, either.

They just kept mooing.

And coming.

And suddenly, with my arms extended and my hands actually pushing on the head of what appeared to be the Queen of the Cows and my fly rod tucked under my right armpit, I was pushed gently off the gravel bar.

And into the North Platte River.

The pool where the trout were still rising—you have not really seen big trout rising until you've seen them rising at eye level as you float past them—was about eight feet deep, I estimated. I estimated my personal height at, well, less than eight feet. And so I floated. Right up to my chin. The cows drank madly from the very spot where I'd been standing just moments before, seemingly oblivious to the floating, screaming human now headed downstream.

I dragged myself out on another gravel bar on the opposite side of the river about thirty feet downstream, gasping for breath because the cold water had rushed in through the chest region of my waders and had reached all the way to the testicle region. I stripped off the waders and my socks and my long underwear and stood there for a moment, thankful that I had not joined that small list of people who have been killed by brown cows.

I was also thankful that the gravel bar I was now standing on contained several baseball-size rocks which—I wish I was making this up, but I am not—I began launching at the cows while shouting "You sons of bitches!"

Maturity has not always been my strong suit.

The third rock hit a cow squarely on the side of the head and it mooed in what seemed like some pain, and then, standing in my wet boxer shorts alongside a wild river in Wyoming, I felt terribly, terribly sorry.

Specifically, sorry I wasn't able to kick the cow in the ass as she scrambled up the bank and went lurching through the field with her mooing gang of sons-of-bitches friends.

It's been more than twenty years since the cows tried to kill me in Wyoming, and I cannot begin to tell you how much steak I have eaten since then. I'm guessing it's been a ton or two. And wherever I go, I ask for Wyoming beef.

I should probably grow up.

The Fourth-Best Day of My Life

The fourth-best day of my life occurred on October 5, 1987.

The three best days were November 28, 1985, March 3, 1989, and May 28, 1992—the days my children were born.

(If I had to list my fifth-best day, it would probably be that giddy day in June of 1978 when, while working as a reporter for United Press International, I was standing in a crowded Los Angeles County courthouse when actress Farrah Fawcett walked by and accidentally brushed against my ass. And if my older son's grades don't improve pretty soon, his birthday could be replaced by what I like to call the "Farrah Fawcett ass incident.")

———

RICH TOSCHES

Anyway, back to the fourth-best day of my life.

It began about thirty miles east of Saratoga, Wyoming, when I shot a huge mule-deer buck. I hadn't "bagged" a deer or elk in a decade, in part because after spotting them in the woods, I'd almost always trip while sprinting toward them with the Wal-Mart shopping sack.

Anyway, I had the big deer in the back of the truck by 10 A.M. and by noon found myself standing knee-deep in a remote section of the North Platte River, fly rod in hand and not a cow within ten miles.

And for three hours I caught wild rainbows and browns, perhaps fifty or more, all of them full of a majestic fight and spirit that said, "We are native Wyoming trout, and it's not out of the question that someday one of us could be elected governor!"

I think that's what they said.

But the point is, the trout hit dry flies at a breathtaking rate, sometimes on consecutive casts, never more than a half-dozen casts before a fish struck, rushing at the Tricos and baetis and even caddis with amazing energy. In one memorable incident, I was changing flies when a gust of wind blew the line and newly attached Trico out of my hands. It landed about three feet upstream and was dragged quickly downstream by the leader, making it appear that the fly was water-skiing. And a fifteen-inch brown chased it almost to my leg and inhaled it. (I mean the Trico. I still have my leg.)

For about thirty seconds I had to fight this fish with the fly rod tucked under my arm as I struggled with my magnifying-reading glasses sliding off my nose and simultaneously trying to get my fly box closed and back into a vest pocket.

Somehow, I eventually netted what I'm guessing was the brown-trout version of Dan Quayle.

Rob and my other hunting/fishing friends had gathered along the riverbank at some point and were watching as I connected with trout after trout after trout as tens of thousands of brilliant gold cottonwood leaves rustled along the banks.

And for one day, one magical day that all fly anglers dream of, I was the "Lord of the River."

This should not be confused with either *River Dance* or *Lord of the Dance*—those show in which popular Irish dancers slap their feet around in such a frenzy that eventually the bottles of whiskey *and* the potatoes fall out of their pants and go sliding across the stage.

(That, of course, was just a stupid stereotype joke and I hereby issue this apology: I am sorry for my insensitive comment. Not all Irishmen carry potatoes in their pants.)

And Then There's Saratoga Lake

(Note: I would have come up with a catchier title for this final story about the fantastic fishing around Saratoga, Wyoming, but frankly, I used up nearly all of my creative talent on "The Cows Are Trying to Drown Me" and am now struggling just to slap a name on these stories.)

Saratoga Lake sits just on the edge of the town, nestled among tall grasses and juniper bushes and high-desert sage. We'd been directed to the lake by the owner of the Great Rocky Mountain Outfitters fly shop in town. We gave him the prerequisite $35 each, grabbed the flies he forced us to purchase, and headed for the lake.

The flies were tiny mysis shrimp. The fishing was amazing. Huge trout cruised the weed beds edging out from the shoreline, occasionally making themselves known with gigantic splashes and swirls as they moved through clusters of the shrimp. Sometimes we'd see them moving along under the surface, browns and rainbows of five and eight and even ten pounds. My hands shook as I tied on my first fly, partly because of the presence of the giant, startling fish but mostly, I believe, because of the enormous amounts of George Dickel whiskey we had consumed in the cabin the night before.

I laid out about thirty feet of line on my first cast and began a slow, twitching retrieve that perfectly mimicked the natural movement of the shrimp. Which was a good thing, because "slow and twitching" was all my hands were capable of. With all due respect to the George Dickel distillery and what I'm sure is its battery of lawyers, it's a fine whiskey unless you have any plans for the following day—such as getting up.

Anyway, I had retrieved the fly perhaps five or ten feet when the fish struck, a heavy, surging tug that stripped line from my hands and had me making loud, whooping noises. The five-weight rod bent heavily and from my left someone shouted, "Keee-rist! What is that?"

(Turns out it was one of my cabin mates and George Dickel drinking partners on the shore who had coughed up something, something that had apparently been dislodged from his small intestine by the whiskey, and he was now staring at it.)

The battle went on for almost ten minutes, long screeching runs followed by heavy, sulking head shaking as the monster trout tried to get rid of the fly. When he appeared on the surface about ten feet away, I greeted him with the magical words a fly angler saves for these moments of complete and utter exhilaration:

"Holy shit!"

*   *   *

I had about half of the fish in my net a few moments later, stumbling backward toward the shore as I gently dragged him along on the surface, a rainbow trout of astounding proportions. My rear end plopped down on a clump of grass on the shore, and after removing the tiny shrimp from the corner of his mouth, I held him for a moment on the lake surface. I took out a tape measure and gasped at the number at the end of the fish's tail—twenty-seven inches—and carefully held him in the water as he regained his strength.

When the giant trout swam back into the depths, I could feel my heart pounding like it hadn't pounded in years. (See *Farrah Fawcett ass incident*.)

There would be many more fish that pounded our flies in Saratoga Lake over the years. The shrimp patterns were consistent winners, but I also took dozens of big fish on drys and small pheasant-tail nymphs. I never caught another to match that first one, but many were over twenty inches and some measured twenty-three and twenty-four inches—giant, fat, healthy trout.

A year after the initial adventure I brought some older friends from Massachusetts, Bill and Butch and Billy, who is now deceased, to the shores of Saratoga Lake. One day we caught a dozen or more big trout in an hour. Bill Meaden, who had spent a lifetime fly-fishing, called it the greatest day he'd ever had on trout water. Bob "Butch" Butcher smiled nonstop for three hours as the trout crashed his shrimp pattern.

And Billy, who was in his seventies, laughed out loud at the sheer joy of the whole thing.

Billy died a few years later. I can still see him standing on the shore of Saratoga Lake. And I can still hear his laugh that day.

———

RICH TOSCHES

When it's at its best, and sometimes even when it's not, fly-fishing can stamp a permanent memory like that. Days can live forever. For example, I'm betting that today, somewhere in the majestic ranchland near Saratoga, Wyoming, a cow is telling her calf about the day Grandma made a man in big rubber pants go for a swim in the river.

CHAPTER 20

Pontoon Boat Envy

Where Lunkers Lurk

Wading in the creeks and streams and rivers and wading into our lakes and ponds and reservoirs, however, apparently is not enough for the avid fly angler. Many years ago, according to fly-fishing historians, a man, probably named Chuck, stood on the shore of a lake, gazed out at the water, and spoke these prophetic words:

> "Someday we'll find a way to be out there, away from the shore, our gigantic asses submerged as we float around in some kind of tube."

———

And the float tube was born.

Today, it is not uncommon on many trout lakes to see dozens of people bobbing around out there, propelling themselves by kicking swim fins that are attached to their feet, their behinds wedged into an inflated truck-tire tube that is marketed as a "belly boat." We gladly pay $200 or $300 for the privilege of climbing into this contraption so we can float around with the fishes. Although in parts of New Jersey you get to do the same thing for free—as long as you're willing to talk to the FBI and rat on Vinny.

And because we are America, we have taken this concept of floating around in a truck tire to astonishing heights. At the top of the line, they are called personal float craft or pontoon craft and can cost $1,000 or more. My personal favorite is the Dave Scadden Pontoon Craft. I am now looking at an advertisement for this fine product that appeared in the September 2001 edition of *Fly Fisherman* magazine. Let's review this ad.

At the top, the ad screams: HOT, NEW! REVOLUTIONARY! NEW!

(Modern marketing, as you know, is 1 percent new ideas and 99 percent exclamation points.)

Under this herd of exclamation points in the ad, we find the actual name of this "Hot, New! Revolutionary! New!" device.

It is called: Cardiac Canyon.

This name was chosen by the Dave Scadden Co. marketing department over two other fine suggestions: Massive Stroke Craft and Complete Kidney Failure Boat.

Here now, more of the actual wording in what I stress is a fine, well-made fly-fishing pontoon craft that you and your fly-fishing friends will use and enjoy right up until you drown.

"It's revolutionary, eight-piece frame and 49 lb. weight store easily in our 28x28x12 boat pack!"

I believe the first word of that sentence should have been "its," without the apostrophe.

But frankly, as a fly fisherman, if I have to choose between (a) a company that does not dwell on grammar but chooses instead to concentrate its efforts on making a highly dependable personal pontoon boat; or (b) a company that spends its resources on fancy marketing departments and copy editors who produce perfect grammatical advertisements, yet also produces personal pontoon boats that will explode and send me screeching across the lake and over the dam, well, I say you go with that first company.

It's just the way I am.

The ad for the Cardiac Canyon pontoon boat also makes this claim: "Revolutionary 11 ft., 6 in. length."

As you know, for centuries our personal fly-fishing pontoon craft have been either eleven feet long or twelve feet long. The guys with the smaller ones would invariably suffer from what psychiatrists call "pontoon boat envy." The guys with the twelve-footers would walk around with a big arrogant smile on their faces—right up until word got around the bar that they were having trouble "inflating the pontoon," if you know what I mean.

Anyway, we grappled with this monumental problem for a long time before finally someone at the Dave Scadden Co. blurted out this idea: "Hey, I know! Let's make a pontoon boat that's bigger than eleven feet and smaller than twelve feet!"

This caused Dave Scadden himself to jump out of his seat during the board meeting—toppling forward, of course, because he was wearing swim fins—and shout, "Sweet Mary and Joseph! That's revolutionary!"

Another note in the ad proclaims the Cardiac Canyon pontoon

boat, which includes a seat that extends a couple of feet above the pontoons, has "zero wind resistance."

Because I was skeptical of this claim, I contacted the chairman of the physics department at esteemed Harvard University. I asked him whether a personal pontoon boat used by a fly fisherman so he could get away from the shore and thus wouldn't keep getting his woolly bugger stuck in the shrubs and have to lurch around on the shore trying to retrieve the $1.99 fly could, possibly, be designed so as to offer "zero wind resistance."

Being an intellectual, the professor responded with a rhetorical question: "How the $%^* did you get my phone number?"

Then he called me an asshole and hung up.

But the point is, if the Dave Scadden Co. has come up with a design so unbelievably thin and streamlined that it offers absolutely *no wind resistance,* I believe what they have created is swimsuit supermodel Elle MacPherson.

Now there's something I'd like to ride across a lake!

Anyway, most of the guys I know have simple float tubes or belly boats that do, indeed, consist of a truck tire tube. This allows us to get out onto the lake where the lunkers lurk. As a bonus, the truck-tire tube will eventually burst, which causes us to go skimming across the water at breathtaking speeds in a final act of manly thrill seeking before we drown or, as mentioned previously, go flying over the dam.

The float-tube experience begins near the shoreline. Step number one involves pulling on your waders. If you forget this crucial step, you will find yourself sitting in a lake while wearing pants. After the waders are on, you put swim fins on your feet. If used correctly, these will propel you quickly across the water at speeds reaching one-one-hundredth of a mile per hour. As a bonus, they also put an unbelievable amount of stress on the ligaments and tendons in your knees, eventually crippling you and thus keeping you from skiing, which is a *really* stupid sport.

After you've put on your waders and rubber swim fins, you climb into the tube and begin the graceful walk toward the water. There are two popular methods for doing this. The first is to walk forward. This allows the tips of your gigantic swim fins to catch the ground, toppling you face first into the lake. The more preferred method, of course, is to walk backward. Using this approach, the modern angler is able to stumble over something he cannot see and topple into the lake with the back of his head leading the way.

For the few anglers who ever actually get into the lake without having their lungs fill with water, the next step is to kick the swim fins in a manner that allows you to go around and around in circles until it's time to go home. This, as I understand it, is called "whirling disease" and is a big problem on many trout waters.

My favorite experience in one of these float tubes came in 1997 on an outing with my outdoor writer friend, Karl Licis, who, as I mentioned earlier, apparently doesn't like me. The trip brought us to Spinney Mountain Reservoir some sixty miles west of Colorado Springs, Colorado. On the way up Karl mentioned that the place tends to get a "little breezy."

As I was to find out, this was like saying former President Bill Clinton tends to get a "little horny."

After waddling around the shore for a while with my ass wedged into the float tube, picking myself back up a dozen times after tripping over the swim fins and then taking both the tube and the fins off so I could hike back to Karl's truck, where I had left my fly rod, I somehow found myself drifting away.

I caught a nice rainbow, Karl hooked and landed a huge pike, and then the wind came.

The wind came over the mountains and, to borrow a phrase made popular by Kansas trailer-home owners being interviewed on TV after watching their house take off, "sounded like a freight train."

Suddenly I found myself in a tire tube that was riding up the front of four-foot waves and down the other side, into troughs so deep I expected to find Rush Limbaugh feeding in one of them. The wind was howling at 40 and 50 mph, I would learn from the National Weather Service the next day—after I was done choking Karl.

And it was blowing parallel to the shore. No matter how hard I kicked the swim fins, I could not close the gap between myself and land. I was screaming and flailing my arms and kicking as hard as I could as I went past the spot on the shore where he was standing, having apparently anticipated the "little breeze."

As I went sailing past him frantically waving my hand at him, Karl responded by waving back.

I washed up on a point that extended well out into the lake, some one and a half miles from where I was when the typhoon hit. When I crawled out of the float tube, I tried to stand up and went lurching sideways for about thirty feet, my knees aching and my thigh muscles burning and unable to hold my weight. I lay on my side on the gravel for about fifteen minutes thinking about what a wonderful experience this float-tube thing had been.

And wondering if Karl's proctologist would return my landing net.

CHAPTER 21

Tying It All Together

I f you become an avid fly angler, you go through a lot of flies. You lose them in all the typical ways.

Snagged in a bush.

Snagged on a log in the river.

Snagged in the side of that guy's neck after he tried foolishly to move into the pool you were fishing.

At about a buck and a half each, losing flies can get expensive. Eventually, most fly anglers tire of shelling out their hard-earned cash. The exception would be attorneys, who simply pad the billable hours sheet and buy more flies—which they display proudly on a patch

———

of wool they keep on their dorsal fin and go on catching fish the usual way: in their three rows of razor-sharp teeth.

And so now we venture into one of the oldest, most traditional and enjoyable aspects of fly-fishing, a much more enjoyable way to fill our fly box. That's right, during a streamside lunch we take a handful of flies out of our friend's fly box while he's off in the bushes taking a leak.

No, actually, we begin the art of fly-tying.

And instead of *buying* flies, we create our own flies—right after we buy $200 stainless-steel vises, delicate feathers plucked from the groin area of Peruvian mountain sparrows, fur yanked from a cheetah's rump by a swift African tribesman, hooks handmade in Sweden by a man named Sven, who can, in a good week, make two of them, and fly-tying desks made of a certain type of birch that only grows on one hill in a very-hard-to-get-to part of Newfoundland.

By doing that, we will, if we live to the age of 214 and tie flies six days a week, have saved approximately forty-five cents.

Here's just one of hundreds of desks you can purchase to begin tying flies, a desk handmade by the terrific Chilton Co. in Freeport, Maine, and advertised this way:

A FLY TYER'S DREAM

Imagine my surprise when the advertisement went on and on and nowhere did it mention getting a back rub by the Dixie Chicks.

Anyway, the ad says: "Keep things organized and neat with this handsome birch desk and cabinet. Eight large drawers are lined on the bottom with red cedar to naturally protect your wool, fur and feathers from moths."

Nothing displeases me, personally, as much as having hundreds of moths in my wool. Never is this more true than when the wool is my long-underwear bottoms and I am wearing them when the cloud of moths descends from the sky.

This fine fly-tying desk is available, we are told, for $799, plus shipping and handling.

In other words, after you've tied your 350th blue-winged olive, which should take you no more than ten or fifteen years if you have other interests such as A JOB, the damn thing has paid for itself!

Another option is the wonderful fly tyer's desk made by the equally terrific George D. Roberts Co. of St. Louis, a desk available "in three sizes in oak, cherry, walnut or the wood of your choice." (My favorite is the wood from the rare Ply tree.)

This ad says your family will be proud to have this desk prominently displayed in the home and asks: "Why tie alone in a cold, damp basement or back room?"

Why, you might be wondering, would anyone tie flies alone in a cold, damp basement?

I'll tell you why.

Because your wife just found out you spent this kind of money on a friggin' fly-tying desk while her 1986 Dodge Dart keeps sending up a billowing cloud of orange smoke every time she steps on the gas pedal, her best shoes are held together with a tube of Goop, and a month ago you told her that new spatulas are too expensive and she can just turn the kids' pancakes with that broken yardstick that's in the closet.

Anyway, in an effort to make this section on fly tying more realistic, I will now clamp my own high-tech fly-tying vise to my computer desk and actually try to create some of the flies listed in a fly-tying book.

My vise, by the way, is an expensive English-made model hand-crafted and designed to hold even the tiniest hooks in a firm yet delicate way so as not to stress the fine metal of these hooks.

Oh sure, it may look like a clothespin glued to a sheet of wood from the Ply tree, but is NOT.

Okay, the first fly we will tie is called, I am not kidding, the "PMD Cripple." This fly imitates the pale morning dun and, as a bonus, gets those really good parking spaces right in front of the grocery store.

(Yipes. Was that insensitive, or WHAT?)

First, according to the book, we will tie the tail and body from pheasant tail. I will do this as soon as I get Max, my Labrador retriever, to stop shaking it.

Okay, now we'll make the thorax of the insect out of yellow Haretron dubbing. Haretron, as you might guess, is made from a rabbit, or hare.

(Dubbing is what they do to make Britney Spears's voice sound a little less like a cat getting its tail stuck under a rocking chair.)

The wing of the PMD Cripple is where things really get interesting. According to the book, the only material suitable for the wing is "coastal deer hair."

I am not kidding.

And I'm not sure how one gathers coastal deer hair. Although I'm guessing you might just wait on the beach and hope one washes up after being hit by a ship.

So I have made the tail and body from pheasant tail, lightly coated with dog spit, and tied to a No. 14 Tiemco TMC 100 hook, which is made in Japan by a sissy-guy who apparently couldn't hack the twenty-one-hour days in the Toyota factory anymore.

Then I wrapped the yellow Haretron dubbing and finished it

off with the coastal deer hair and voilà . . . I have created what appears to be a good-sized moth.

Perhaps that one was a bit too difficult. I'll try a "Hi-Vis Parachute."

Let's see here. This one—I swear I'm not kidding—will require a Tiemco TMC 101 hook, gray 8/0 thread, and . . . "hackle fibers from a grizzly bear."

(And I thought wrestling that pheasant out of my dog's mouth and yanking a feather out of the bird's ass was a big deal.)

I am reading this fly book, and frankly, I can't seem to find a single fly that can be tied without some degree of danger. The Iso Compara-Nymph, for example, calls for "mallard flank fibers dyed amber." I don't know what kind of company you hang out with, but frankly, I don't want to risk the good-natured ribbing I'd get if any of my friends caught me out in the swamp, rubbing amber dye or, to be honest, rubbing ANYTHING between a mallard's thighs.

Here's the Royal Double Wing, which requires brown elk hair (make sure not to use the *blue* elk hair that is commonly found on older elk, especially the ones living in Miami) and the following material for the wing: "belly hair from a white-tailed deer."

As I understand it, the accepted way to get this wing material is to dig a shallow hole, about six feet long, in a well-marked game trail. Lie down in the hole, facing up. Keep your hands ready. Then, at some time during the fall or early winter, when a white-tailed deer walks over you, reach up quickly toward the belly, grab a handful, and hang on.

(Important Footnote: If it's a big buck and you grab this handful after most of the deer's underbelly has passed by, especially during the rutting season, you'll *really* need to hang on.)

Finally, here's another fly, one that I have actually tied. It's called the Love Bug, a small bead-head emerger created by a noted fly angler and fly tyer who goes by the actual name of Trapper Badovinac. (Legend has it he got his name during college, when he actually chewed off his leg to get away from a blind date.)

Anyway, the Love Bug is tied on a tiny, No. 18-22 Tiemco hook and calls for a wing made of partridge feather. (I nearly killed myself when I fell out of the pear tree.)

And the thorax is made from beaver.

As I said, I've tied this fly. I actually used it once, on a stream near my Colorado home. I caught two nice rainbows in the first half hour. Then a knot broke and the fly was free from the tippet. Later that day, however, it came out of the river, gnawed down forty aspen trees, and built a huge dam.

I'm not kidding.

CHAPTER 22

In Which a Fish Flips Me the Bird

After you've been fly-fishing for a few decades, you start thinking you're pretty good at this sport.

You are not.

If you need proof of this, travel to famous tailwater fisheries such as Colorado's Frying Pan River or Taylor River. Stand at the big pools closest to the dams, put on Polarized sunglasses, and peer into the water. You will see trout that have reached stunning size by feeding on a steady diet of shrimp. (After twenty years of marriage, actress Rhea Perlman, who is married to

---

four-foot-ten-inch actor Danny DeVito, also complains of a "steady diet of shrimp.")

Anyway, I've stood at these fly-fishing meccas and seen the beasts that lurk beneath the water. Rainbows mostly, outlandish trout of five and ten and fifteen pounds. Feeding. Constantly feeding. Moving back and forth in the current to inhale the tiny mysis shrimp that have been sucked from the reservoir and are now rushing from under the dam.

It's October of 1988. Having spent three days hunting elk, I need a break. Mostly, a break from listening to the damn elk bugling or "laughing" as they run away from me. So I find myself along the banks of the Frying Pan, which empties from Ruedi Reservoir, which is named for Ruedolph, the Red Nosed Reindeer. I think.

I start about a mile downstream of the dam and am having quite a good day, hooking and landing eight rainbows before noon, nice fish between fifteen and eighteen inches long. The aspens are a brilliant gold, the air is warm, and life is good.

Then a no-good son of a bitch named Lee shows up. He seems like a decent guy at first. We talk. Then he says if I really want to see some big trout, I should walk up to the pool just beneath the dam.

So I do.

I'm an idiot.

In the pool are trout that are so big it makes you gasp. Thirty inches long and more. Fat. Gigantic tails. And they're feeding. Slashing at things I cannot see, huge mouths opening and closing as they move back and forth in the current. Mysis shrimp, Lee the no-good $%^&*# had told me. White mysis shrimp. I had several in my fly box. Got to use light leaders, Lee had told me. My spools of tippet went all the way down to 8X, which, for those of you unfamiliar with things such as line diameter and tensile strength, is the number-one choice of tippet among those who do not want to ever, ever land a fish because they make their hands all stinky.

I began by tying on shrimp-pattern fly to a section of 5X tippet, which is the lightest I generally use. It breaks if you sneeze too hard while casting. But on this river, at this pool, I might as well have been using clothesline rope.

The massive trout—I could seem them clearly; they fed voraciously within ten feet of me—actually swam *around* the leader to inhale more live shrimp. It was like stepping around your sleeping dog to get to the refrigerator—and then suddenly he awakens and bites you right on the back of the leg to get to the plate of ham you're carrying.

Sorry. I made that last part up.

Anyway, it was obvious the fish, which see hundreds and hundreds of idiots just like me every year sneaking around in L.L. Bean waders, were not interested in anything tied to 5X tippet. So I went to 6X, which the human eye cannot actually see, forcing us to pretend we are tying a knot and then hope for the best.

The trout ignored that, too.

So I went to 7X. On about the fiftieth cast, a monster I figure weighed ten pounds rose from the depths, moved to the shrimp pattern . . . and turned away. About fifty or so casts later, another, slightly smaller trout—probably a child of six pounds or so—did the same thing. They seemed interested—if two fish in one hundred casts can be called "interested"—in the dead-drifting shrimp I was offering.

But that leader . . .

I sat down for a while. I had the pool to myself on this weekday during a splendid Colorado elk season, so didn't risk losing my prime spot. I took out my spool of 8X tippet and laid it down on the ground beside me. I glanced at it, then looked away.

What kind of complete, utter, slobbering, stupid, brain-damaged moron, I thought, would attempt to hook and land one of these huge trout on 8X tippet?

Well, this far into the book I think we all know the answer to that question.

About fifteen minutes later, Dumbo waded back into the Frying Pan.

Trailing behind my fly rod was a long leader. At the end was a No. 18 white-mysis-shrimp fly pattern. Somewhere up ahead of that shrimp was three feet of 8X tippet, which I had tied to the rest of the leader by putting on a pair of thick magnifying eyeglasses and holding the two ends within about an inch of my nose as I fashioned the knot.

As I went back into the river, no matter how I squinted, I could not see the tippet that was attached to my small fly.

I had been trying to hook one of these trout for nearly three hours now.

And then, suddenly, a rainbow rushed at the shrimp. She came from about five feet away as my shrimp approached, her massive tail flicking in the clear water. Her mouth opened. My fly disappeared. I set the hook.

Often, it's hard to measure time. I recall watching Neil Armstrong poised on the final step of the *Eagle's* ladder after it had touched down on the moon in 1969. It seemed like Neil stayed on that step for a long, long time. It was about ten seconds.

My second marriage lasted fourteen years. It seemed like 1,500.

And I believe I had that trout on for about a minute that warm autumn day in the Frying Pan River in 1988. It was probably five or ten seconds. She moved to the left, and my five-weight rod bowed and strained. She moved back to the right and a bit upstream, and my reel sang. She came back downstream, to within maybe ten feet of me.

Then—and I'm pretty sure about this part—I think she gave me the finger.

The next thing I knew, some twenty feet of line had been stripped from my reel and then the weightless, slack line was drifting back downstream. She was gone. I never had a chance. None at all, really. It was like tying kite string to the back of Senator Ted Kennedy's belt, holding on to the other end, and pointing him toward an open bar.

So convincingly beaten was I that I did the same thing, with the same mysis-shrimp pattern and the same three-foot length of 8X tippet, *only five more times that day.*

Did I mention that I'm an idiot?

All five ended the same way the first encounter had. I'm sure the tiny barbless flies were easily dislodged from the gigantic trouts' lips when they returned to the bottom of the pool and gave a few shakes of their big heads.

That night, back at our elk-hunting cabin, I opened a bottle of whiskey and had a long drink. Then I started a grand blaze in the fireplace, put my feet up on a table, leaned back in my chair, and let out a contented sigh.

Then I threw that $%^&*# spool of 8X tippet right into the fire.

CHAPTER 23

Dave, the Dress, and the Brown Midge

My second encounter with ridiculously large trout took place on the Taylor River, below Taylor Reservoir just north of the town of Gunnison, Colorado. It was even worse, in the sense that it was exactly the same as the encounter on the Frying Pan River eight years earlier, except it lasted two days instead of just one.

It was the autumn of 1996. Once again, elk hunting was the excuse for a few days of fly-fishing. The Gunnison elk herd was elusive, running just barely ahead of me in the forest and, through some uncanny knack honed by centuries of being hunted, leaving behind piles of four-week-old droppings.

So after three days I quit and picked up my fly rod. I knew of the pool of monster trout beneath the Taylor Dam. After a few years of living in Colorado, I had heard the quiet, muffled whispers in my local fly shop.

Rainbow trout.

Fifteen pounds and bigger.

Dave the night sales guy sometimes dresses in women's clothes.

Perhaps I heard too much. Nevertheless, I decided to go to the pool and have myself a good look-see, as they say in some rural areas and, of course, all of Arkansas.

The pool was deeper than the one on the Frying Pan, and the fish weren't as easy to spot. But if you sat high on the bank above the pool, they'd emerge from the darkness once in a while. I saw rainbow trout larger than any I'd seen on the Frying Pan. If you don't believe me, the same September 2001 issue of *Fly Fisherman* magazine that I have mentioned earlier has, on page 60, a photo.

The photo shows a man, perhaps in his early thirties, kneeling near the bank in the pool on the Taylor River. In his right hand is a rainbow trout's tail. In his left hand, which is about twenty inches away from his right hand, is a rainbow trout's stomach. Well beyond that left hand is the rest of the trout's stomach region, along with the gills and the head. It is, apparently, the same trout, very much alive and about to be returned to the water, the caption tells us.

The man is not identified in the caption. This is because of his desire to stay out of the spotlight and, of course, because he knows the rest of us who fly-fish would find him and try to choke him. The caption reads: "Tough trout, such as this 10-plus pound Taylor River rainbow, are seldom easy to catch."

The magazine editors chose that carefully worded sentence because the word "Duh!" would not have filled the white space beneath the photo.

Back to October of 1996.

Having watched my spool of 8X tippet burn in the fireplace of the elk-hunting cabin eight years earlier—I would have thrown that $%^&*@ Lee into the fireplace, too, but he had the sense not to come around—the lightest tippet I now carried was a spool of Rio-brand 6X, which has a breaking point of 3.2 pounds.

Although I think it's good stuff, several years ago they made a feature-length film about a guy who kept snapping off nice trout with this brand of leader material and because he was a whiny, yuppy kind of guy, refused to believe it was his fault. The film was called *Blame It On Rio*.

Sorry.

So I got into the Taylor pool and watched these submarines rising to the surface, feeding not on mysis shrimp but apparently on, well, on nothing. No matter how close I got to the surface of the water, without an insect screen to capture and analyze the bugs, I could not see anything that would be causing these giants to sip from the surface.

Midges?

Here we will take a brief side trip into the world of midges. In fly-fishing magazines, midges are often photographed lying on coins as a way to show the smallness of them, if that's a word. You can fit dozens of them on a dime.

I've tried many times to fish with these midges, but on the first cast the dime always sails off into the shrubs.

Okay, enough of that side trip.

My fly box contained dozens of midges, red ones and black ones, all so small I had to pick them out with the tip of my forceps, which are delicate stainless-steel pliers used by fly anglers to remove hooks from fish and by surgeons for the obvious purpose: to pick a golf tee out of their bag on the first tee as you sit in their office miles away, reading a 1968 edition of *Reader's Digest*.

Anyway, I picked out a red midge I believe was a size 24, which is really small. For the rest of that day the huge rainbows in the Taylor River alternated between totally ignoring the red midges and totally ignoring the black midges. They were feeding on something, though. As the sun dipped below the mountains, another angler stopped by.

"They've been hitting brown midges," he said.

I wondered if anyone would find out if I threw him into the river.

Then I wondered if he was related to that $%^%&*# Lee over on the Frying Pan River.

I came back at about 10 A.M. the next day. I had a dozen brown midges that I'd purchased the previous evening in Gunnison, about twenty-five miles away.

I hooked two trout before noon.

One stripped nearly all of my fly line from the reel, sulked across the pool near the opposite bank for about forty-five seconds, and then the fly came loose. He jumped once on the way over. I'd guess he weighed seven or eight pounds.

Energized by this roaring success of having a trout on my line for nearly minute, I began making more drifts with the tiny brown midge. At about 11:30, all hell broke loose.

The fish took the fly just under the surface and a large area—a very large area—of water turned white. He ran upstream into the heaviest flow of the river, then back to the other end of the pool some fifty yards away. This took approximately one second.

Then the fish headed back upstream and jumped. Drool actually escaped my mouth and ran down my chin. I no longer wanted to catch this fish. I just didn't want him to hurt me. If the first fish weighed seven pounds, well, this one was bigger. Much bigger. Maybe twice as big.

He kept making great spurts back and forth from the front of the pool to the back and from the opposite bank to within fifteen feet of my shaking knees, at which time I'd stand perfectly still because I was afraid he would notice me and attack me.

The tiny fly came loose after a while. The line just went dead and that was that.

My first thought? I looked at the net dangling from my vest, and I smiled. If the fish had stayed on, if somehow he had been subdued on this 6X tippet—my best hope seemed to be that maybe he'd have a heart attack—the net was a bit too small anyway. I think I might have gotten part of his head into it.

So now, speaking to you as a fly fisherman who has stood in some of the West's most prolific waters and come away with nothing to show for it except some vivid memories, snapped leaders, and a fear of large trout, I can say this:

6X.

That's the ticket.

CHAPTER 24

Snuggling with Misty Fiords

E ventually, this itch that is fly-fishing must be severely scratched, leaving you with quite a rash and a lot of ointments from the pharmacy, although I may be thinking of poison sumac.

The point is, after a while, if your blood runs thick with a love for this sport and your spine is made of graphite, your fly-fishing thoughts turn to the Big One.

I'm talking, of course, about Alaska—our thirty-fourth state, if you don't count West Carolina or East Dakota and I, personally, do not.

I was still living in Los Angeles when the first urge struck to fish in Alaska. I began planning a trip using three important criteria: the quality of the fishing, knowledgeable guides, and of course, finding someone else to pay for the entire thing.

I cannot stress enough the importance of that last one. A week at a decent lodge in Alaska will run you anywhere between $5,000 and $1.5 million, depending on whether or not you bring Ivana Trump with you. My first trip to Alaska or "America's Dairyland" was funded in part by *Sports Illustrated* magazine, which paid a handsome sum for an article on my adventure. As I understand it, the nation's premier sports magazine had quite a bit of money left over that year because of a high-level executive decision that said, basically, instead of hiring expensive experts as they'd done in the past, from now on the anemic swimsuit models would be responsible for brushing the sand out of their *own* butt cracks.

Anyway, the first of my three trips to Alaska brought me and my friends Larry Mascari and *L.A. Times* photographer Mike Meadows to the southern Alaska village of Ketchikan, which is a native Inuit fishing term and means, literally, "I have caught a can." We landed shortly after noon at the Ketchikan International Airport, which consists of a sandbar and a gift shop, and soon found ourselves at our lodge alongside the Misty Fiords National Monument. Misty Fiords, ironically, was also my high-school girlfriend, and while she was not an actual "national monument," I found out years later she was a "local treasure"—at least among about forty other guys in the senior class.

We walked down to the docks beneath our lodge, and as we gazed out across Alaska's famed Inland Passage—a maze of islands, seals, and majestic bird-poop-covered rocks—a group of killer whales surfaced no more than a hundred yards offshore, sending sprays of water high into the air by blowing air out of the holes in the tops of their heads, just the way Dan Quayle does when you force him to try to spell "potato."

The killer whales, we were told, were chasing salmon, which they would herd into big schools and then devour. I'd come a long way and was spending quite a bit of someone else's money to catch these salmon, so I began cursing and throwing large rocks at the whales before Larry and Mike wrestled me to the ground. In a tribute to this bravery in the face of the killer whales, a local Inuit elder who had been watching the whole thing said, in his native tongue, *"Terifik weik e mo, lare kirlaa"*—which I later found out meant, "Terrific, we get to spend a week with Mo, Larry, and Curly."

On the first day we set out onto the sound in an aluminum boat in search of the salmon. This was going to be quite difficult because, due to pollution and overfishing, there are only about 987 trillion salmon that swim into Alaskan waters each year. We were after king salmon, which look different from the dozen or so other species of salmon mostly because of the crown on their heads. And the British accent.

It didn't take long for us to hook into the powerful fish, with the three of us whooping and hollering as the thirty- and forty-pound salmon streaked across the calm sea. I was the only one using a fly rod, an eight-weight fiberglass rod that bent and shuddered with each screeching run by a salmon. It would often take as long as twenty minutes to subdue a big king on this rod, with Mike and Larry using spinning gear, reeling in each fish and then taking a nice nap while they waited for me.

But if you've ever hooked a big fish, a really big fish such as a striped bass or big bluefish or a king salmon, on a fly rod, you know why I was using this equipment and not spinning gear for my battle with the streaking fish.

That's right: I believed I was better than my two friends.

The highlight of the trip for me came a few days later when we boarded a float plane known as a Beaver—I tripped over the two big front teeth as I was climbing in—and headed into the remote bush country of Alaska, where, we were told, we'd find hungry trout in a pristine lake. The pilot was Charlie Ward, who was seventy-four years old and said he shuttled anglers into this remote country all the time, which made me confident. Making me a little less confident was the fact that the seventy-four-year-old Charlie also claimed he had, earlier that morning, dropped off President Millard Fillmore at the same lake.

The trip went well, though, Charlie swooping his Beaver low over the endless green forests before banking sharply and settling the pontoons onto the surface of a place he called Salmon Lake. I asked what kind of fish were in Salmon Lake and he said, seriously, "Trout."

I grinned and asked him what kind of fish we'd find in "Trout Lake."

He said he didn't know any place called Trout Lake and then he ignored me for three hours.

Alaskans are funny like that.

Charlie guided the plane toward the shore and we all hopped out in our hip boots. Charlie told Larry to "hold the plane for a minute" and handed him a long rope that was hooked to one of the pontoons. About ten minutes later—after I was pretty much done crying and screaming about how the bears would eat us and we'd never see our homes again—Charlie reappeared along the shoreline, carrying a very large rock.

He came back through the shallow water with the rock, plunked it onto one of the pontoons, grabbed the rope, wrapped it several times around the rock, and then dropped the boulder into the lake.

"The thing about float planes," said old Charlie Ward, who was not smiling at all, "is they never stop until you tie 'em to something."

We were speechless in the presence of such a wise man, so we just shut up and started fishing.

We had come to a stop near a gravel bar that extended perhaps two hundred feet into the lake, with deep water on both sides. I tied on a bright orange streamer, added a split shot to get it down a bit, and began casting.

And caught twenty-six trout on my first twenty-six casts. I am not kidding.

The trout were called dolly varden, a brightly colored species common in extreme northern waters such as in Alaska. (Dolly varden can be differentiated from Dolly *Parton* quite easily: when Dolly Parton heads upstream on her annual spawning run, she leaves two enormous trenches in the gravel on the river bottom. At least that's what the old Inuits say.)

If fly-fishing can be too easy—and it cannot—then this would have been that day. I caught trout with a fast retrieve and a slow retrieve. I caught trout when I just let the fly sink. I caught them deep and near the surface. For about fifteen minutes, I actually switched the rod to my left hand, made a series of feeble, awkward casts of about twenty feet, and caught trout that way, too. It was fun, but after a few hours I longed for a good, old-fashioned skunking, at least a cast or two without getting a sharp jolt from trout that had, apparently, not had anything to eat in about two years.

I wanted to catch nothing!

But I couldn't.

By noon, I estimated I'd made 150 casts and caught perhaps 125 trout. We released them all, so I began thinking that maybe there were only two or three trout in Salmon Lake, but they were *really* aggressive. I suggested this to Charlie Ward and his brow furrowed as he thought about it for a few seconds. Then he walked about thirty feet farther away from me and never said another word.

To my right, Larry and Mike had been catching trout, too, on their spinning rods. Larry was now making casts backward, over his head, and reeling the lure in that way and hooking a trout on most every cast. Mike was casting sideways, staring at the lush shoreline and a Forest Service cabin nestled in the woods, and was catching fish without looking.

Eventually we took a break and headed for the shore and the cabin, just to check it out. This plan was aborted as we got to shore and saw, in the soft muddy beach, footprints that were made either by a grizzly bear or Los Angeles Lakers' center Shaquille O'Neal.

(If it was indeed the great NBA basketball star, I'd really suggest he start trimming his toenails more often.)

The bear tracks were enormous, each one the same size as if a man had put his hands together, fingers to wrist, and pressed them into the soil. I know this because I did just that. As I stood there in the Alaskan wilderness, gazing in awe at the tracks in the mud, I had just one thought: "Man, I've got to wash this shit off my hands."

With a creepy feeling that perhaps I was being watched from the dense, dark forest by a thousand-pound bear, I scurried back into the lake toward the plane and tried to get over my uneasiness by catching about six hundred more trout before Charlie said it was time to go.

The Beaver shook as it roared across the lake and suddenly we were in the air again, headed for the lodge. Before I knew it I was back in Los Angeles. But even today I smile with the knowledge that on the final day of my first trip to Alaska, on one marvelous day in the bush of Alaska, I was almost as good a fisherman as those Vietnamese guys with the dynamite.

CHAPTER 25

Father and Son Share a Moment at the Dump

F or every little boy who falls in love with fly-fishing there is a man who made it possible, a kind and gentle man who saw the flame and kindled it. For me, it was a guy who went by the name Lucky and hung out near the liquor store in my hometown and always asked me to rub his feet.

No, really, for me it was my father, Nick. He never fly-fished a day in his life, looking at the delicate nine-foot rod and thinking "Now there's something you're gonna slam in the damn car door, for chrissakes!"

But my father was always behind me. In my pursuit

———

of sports and my pursuit of writing and, frankly, in my pursuit of anything. He was a newspaper editor in Massachusetts for four decades and gave me my first job, which consisted of scraping the sticky paper off the composing room floor with a putty knife. That was thirty-eight years ago.

He still owes me $24.75.

Today he's retired, spending part of each day reading several newspapers, clipping out articles, and sending them to me in the fervent belief that I might find a way to change a word here and there and turn them into my own columns for my newspaper in Colorado Springs so I could be out of the office by noon every day.

He is a wise, wise man.

And when he did indeed purchase that $15 fly rod from his friend Porky Ferrara—okay, I didn't steal it—he backed up the gesture by looking at his goofy twelve-year-old kid the next day and asking "So now what?"

And then he'd drive me to the lake or the pond where I learned how to catch bluegills on a popper or perhaps fall off the dam when the trout struck the dry fly, and later to the West River, where he'd drop me off with my fly rod and my waders and offer words of encouragement such as "Don't drown, for chrissake!"

Sometimes he'd stay and watch—mesmerized, I think, by the sight of his young boy and the graceful motion of the fly rod, the line slicing through the air alongside a New England stream. You could sense the emotion in his voice when he'd shout, "For chrissakes, you're gonna put your eye out with that thing!"

And then he'd leave, probably heading back to the newspaper office for a few hours of work as I stayed and learned the graceful art of fly-fishing.

———

RICH TOSCHES

And most of the time he'd remember to come back and pick me up.

The summer that I got the fly rod, my father asked if I'd like to take a trip with him. Maybe we'd drive up to Maine, he said. And so he bought a huge blue-and-white canvas tent, stuffed it into the trunk of his 1967 Mercury—the fly rod had a safe spot on the backseat—and the two of us left on a ten-day road trip, an adventure that still lingers in my mind today, a magical journey of a young boy and a father who didn't know it when they set out that first day, but who were linked by a powerful bond: Neither of them had any idea how to put up a tent.

The trip brought us north out of Boston along the rugged coast and into Portland, where we turned inland through Lewiston to the town of Mexico—yes, there is an actual place called Mexico, Maine—where we stopped for lunch. We both had the special: moose burritos.

It was right after lunch that we came upon the most exciting thing I had ever seen that did not have a centerfold stapled into the middle of it. It was the Androscoggin River, which combines the native Maine Indian words *Andro* ("land") and *scoggin* ("that L.L. Bean hasn't purchased yet").

The Androscoggin was wider and deeper and faster than any river I had ever seen. It was wide enough that I could not throw a stone across it, although I kept trying until the guy fly-fishing on the opposite shore yelled, "Hey, you little bastard!"

I had no clue whatsoever as to how to fly-fish such a place, a river fast enough and deep enough that I knew only one thing: If I even tried to put my waders on, signaling that I was going to enter the water, my father would have tackled me and thrown me into the trunk with the tent.

———

So I left the waders in the car and rigged up my fly rod, choosing a large black woolly bugger and adding a couple of split shot. I cast and cast for more than an hour without a strike, and then, suddenly, as the streamer swung toward the bank in the heavy current, the rod doubled and nearly came out of my hands. A huge fish moved out into the current and headed downstream, and because I had never felt anything so powerful, I clamped my fingers onto the fly line and heard the eight-pound test leader snap.

It had all happened so fast I hadn't even yelled. I walked back to the car, where my father had a map opened on the hood and told him I'd lost one.

"Yeah?" he asked, looking up. "You probably horsed him."

Ah, "horse this" I was thinking, although I did not actually say that to him. I know that because I am still alive, writing this book.

But as I took the fly rod apart and set it on the backseat and climbed back into the front with my dad, my hands still trembled from that brief encounter with a big trout. As we headed out of the town of Mexico and turned onto Highway 142, passing through the small Maine towns of Carthage and Madrid, I remember having this thought—a powerful thought that would lead me into a lifetime of passionate fly-fishing: "Mexico? Carthage? Madrid? Where the hell are we?"

Anyway, we drove on in the Mercury, which was so big we could have pitched tent in it before we'd left the house. Turns out that wouldn't have been a bad idea. In the late afternoon we pulled into the town of Rangeley, which my dad said he'd found earlier on the map and had actually been *trying* to find. I believed him, which was quite a milestone in our relationship.

I'd doubted him on all travel-related matters since a few years earlier when, on a car trip to Florida with three kids stuffed in the backseat, he ran out of gas on a Georgia cotton plantation. After walking quite a distance to a house and finding no one home—he let me walk along with him despite the fact I was only eight, probably in case they had a big dog—he left a five-dollar bill under a rock on the doorstep and filled a big can with gasoline from a pump near the barn.

After the long walk back, he poured the gasoline into the tank and cranked up the Pontiac. I can still remember turning in the backseat to watch the billowing cloud of black smoke that poured from the exhaust pipe as he drove away that day—and reminding myself that when I got big and had my own car, I would never, ever pour two gallons of diesel fuel into it like my daddy had just done.

I told him later that I saw the word *diesel* handwritten on the pump by the barn, but didn't know what it meant. My dad, kind and understanding at all times, was even more so in critical times such as this. When I told him about seeing that "diesel" word on the pump, I remember him looking at me with those understanding eyes and saying "Jesus Christ, you coulda said something, for chrissakes, dammit to hell!"

Somehow, we made it to Miami, where we spent two terrific weeks, a million memories tucked away in the mind—although for me, about 900,000 of those memories are of watching my father walk along the beach dressed in shorts, black shoes, and black socks.

Anyway, we were in Maine now and pulled into the town of Rangeley during the late afternoon. We stopped at the general store in the little town and bought a couple of sodas. Dad explained to the man behind the counter that we were on a fishing and camping trip. Dad inquired about nearby campgrounds and then asked what there might be to do around town.

"Well," the old man said from behind the counter. "You could go out to the dump and watch the beahs!"

This was Mainese, and meant "bears."

I thought this was a great idea: Let's take the twelve-year-old awkward kid down to the dump to play with the bears.

First, however, there was the simple matter of pitching the tent. So we worked together, both of us huffing and puffing and pulling on this and pulling on that, and surprisingly, within half an hour we had the tent out of the trunk.

We spread it on the ground at the campsite, turning it so the door faced the picnic table. Then dad looked at the gigantic pile of aluminum poles on the ground. Then he looked at me. Then we both looked back at the pile of tent poles. If we had any sense at all, we would have stuffed everything back into the trunk and gone home.

We started messing around with the poles, which slid in and out of other poles and went through Flap A and connected to Center Pole D and Awning Support F—although a lot of that information came the following week when we got home and read the instruction booklet, which *someone* had left in the basement.

I still have that blue-and-white tent. It's in my garage, in the original box. And almost every summer my kids make me take it out and we set it up in the backyard and they sleep in it.

I've told them the history of the tent, and now, whenever we begin setting it up, one of my two lovely sons will say, "Look, I'm Grandpa!" and then he'll kick the pile of poles across the yard and yell, "Dammit to hell!"

Oh, how we laugh.

———

RICH TOSCHES

Anyway, somehow my dad and I got the tent set up. It took about three hours. And at dusk, with camp set, we got back into the car and headed for the Rangeley Town Dump, which was about five miles up a dirt road. And within ten minutes of our arrival, the black bears came out of the woods. Six of them.

My father, Mr. Newspaper Guy, reached into the backseat and pulled out his always ready camera, which did not have any type of telephoto lens, and said I should get out and take some pictures.

I am not kidding.

Once I was outside, with the bears some fifty feet away rifling through the garbage, my father, who stayed in the Mercury, actually said this:

"Get closer!"

A few weeks later, the *Milford Daily News* ran a photograph of bears at a dump in Rangeley, Maine. The credit line read *"Daily News* photo by Richard Tosches." In the photo, one of the bears was very close and you could see it holding its head up, sniffing the air.

Almost as if he had caught the scent of urine in a twelve-year-old kid's pants.

We stayed near Rangeley for three days and discovered gigantic Rangeley Lake. I caught a few trout on my fly rod, Dad caught a few more with his spinning outfit, and we ate trout over the campfire at night. I do not like the taste of trout. I have not eaten one since that night in Maine in 1967. In the years since, we've had a lot of conversations about this idea of catch-and-release. Dad still keeps a trout or two when he fishes and I'm okay with that. But he cannot understand why I release every trout I catch.

"They're good eatin'," he'll say. "Why the hell would anyone go fishing if they won't eat 'em?"

I tell him I do it because I love being in the water, that I love the feeling of being in pristine places where wild trout swim, that I love watching a big trout rise to the surface and sip the tiny fly, perhaps one I have created myself, and feeling the thrill of the fight on the delicate fly rod. I tell him I love knowing that if I do everything just right, I get to watch a large rainbow slide into my net.

"Yeah," he'll say, in that kind and caring way. "I guess I know what you mean.

"Although you could still eat him."

CHAPTER 26

Call Me Ishmael

I would like to pick up the telephone each and every day for the rest of my parents' lives and call them so I could thank them for all they've done for me, and for kindling the fire that became my passion for this sport called fly-fishing. Although quite frankly, after about a month of this, I'm guessing my father would get his phone bill and shout, "Where'd all these collect calls come from, for chrissakes?"

But on my first trip to Alaska with my friends Larry and Mike, I thought about how much my mom and dad meant to me. And I sat on a rock in the majesty that surrounded me and I had the following thought:

"Good God, grizzly-bear scat tastes awful!"

Then I spit it out and looked around to see if anyone had been watching me.

Seriously, another thought I had on my first trip to Alaska was that somehow, someway, I had to bring my father to that stunning land.

A few years later I did.

Although technically, if you're the kind of person who has to factor in who paid for what, he took *me*.

He arrived in Los Angeles after a flight from Boston and we left the next day, headed for Anchorage on Alaska Airlines. My father is not what you'd call "crazy" about flying, in the sense that he believes every plane he ever gets on will "crash" into a remote part of a "forest" where he, as the only survivor, will be eaten by "squirrels."

But as we looked out through the airport terminal window and saw the gigantic face of an Eskimo painted on the tail section of the Alaska Airlines jet, I could tell his confidence level was at an all-time high by the way he said, "What the hell kind of picture is that to put on an airplane?"

We got on anyway, and in a few hours the plane began its descent into the Anchorage airport, which is surrounded by towering mountains, a descent that basically involves the pilot turning off the engines and allowing the plane to drop faster than the pants of a former president who we will just call Bill.

Dad loved this part of the trip.

Today, some fifteen years later, I'm guessing the FBI crime-lab people could still find Alaska Airlines seat fibers under his fingernails.

RICH TOSCHES

But the best part was yet to come. This was the part in which we had to crawl through the door of a tiny airplane for a forty-five-minute flight to the lodge, the plane zooming over the spectacular Kenai Peninsula as the giant rubber band unwound and spun the propeller.

The pilot had put Dad and me in the two backseats of the nine-passenger jet, aware of the need for perfect weight balance on the light craft and, of course, instinctively knowing that if we were seated anywhere near the door, my father would, at some point, try to open it and leap out.

But everything went just fine and soon we arrived at the airport in a town called Homer, which was named for the ancient Greek writer Homer and philosopher Ulysses.

We were greeted at the airport by a representative of the Ninilchik Lodge and soon found ourselves in a van, passing lush forests and breathtaking views of Cook Inlet, which was named for the explorer who discovered the area: Homer.

I cannot begin to write the words that could possibly describe the setting of the Ninilchik Lodge except to say it sits right on the beach at the edge of a forest of towering pines, the gentle waves of the inlet lapping rhythmically on the gravel-lined shore as eagles soar overhead. It evokes a feeling of great serenity and yet at the same time an adrenaline rush of adventure sweeps over all who have ever set foot in this amazing spot.

Anyway, my father and I stood there for several moments without saying a word, taking in the most incredible view either of us had ever seen—if you don't count a black bear chasing a kid through a dump as his father shouts, "Don't drop the goddamn camera!!!!"

This would be our home for the next five days. Beyond the beach, out there in the emerald-colored waters of Cook Inlet, swam tens of thousands of king salmon—fish that had spent three or four years growing to outlandish size in the rich waters of the Pacific and had returned in a remarkable display of determination to the place they were created, thirty- and forty- and fifty-pound fish which now had only one thing on their minds: avoiding getting a mouthful of cheap ashes flicked relentlessly over the side of a boat by this strange creature who kept saying "Look, it's another eagle, for chrissakes!"

We made our way to our room and stowed our gear, which included the fiberglass Shakespeare Wonder Rod that my father had purchased for me some twenty years earlier. The Wonder Rod had seen many remarkable things in those two decades—from a salmon from hell in a small creek that emptied into the waters of Green Bay, Wisconsin, to the furious bonito of Redondo Beach, California.

The Wonder Rod, however, had never seen anything quite like what it was about to see in these waters of Alaska.

(Here I briefly considered writing the rest of the book from the perspective of the Shakespeare Wonder Rod, but was dissuaded from this approach by my literary agent, Chip MacGregor, who said in his calm and soothing way, "Are you a moron, or what?")

Later in the evening, after watching more than a dozen eagles land on the beach, we gathered at the dinner table at the Ninilchik Lodge with a few other guests and learned about the history of the place. Ninilchik, we were told, is a native word meaning, well, it means something. I should have paid more attention, but the history session made me flash back to my carefree days of high school and I found myself looking out the window and daydreaming—a daydream that ended suddenly when the lodge owner shrieked, leaped out of his seat, pulled a thumbtack out of his ass, and spent the rest of the meal staring pointedly at me.

We would be fishing, we were told, from large aluminum boats. We would troll and drift mostly, which was the accepted way of taking these heavyweights. But there would be opportunities to cast a fly, too, and I was excited by that prospect.

Not as excited, I would find out, would be the other guys in the boat—who didn't much care to have a gigantic, brightly colored streamer fly with a huge hook whipped back and forth just over their heads by a guy who had, during the wildlife discussion at that first dinner, asked, "So, like, do the birds that *have* hair make fun of the bald eagles?"

Turns out there would be no fly-fishing from the boats, but the Wonder Rod would have its moments.

Anyway, after dinner we stood on the beach and watched the midsummer Alaska sun try to set, but it never really did. To the west, across Cook Inlet, stood two active volcanoes named Iliamna and Redoubt. Iliamna had been spitting smoke for months, and each night the sun would briefly dip beneath the chain of mountains and the volcanoes, the fading sunlight turning the volcanic smoke and sparkling water into an unforgettable painting of red and gold light.

At noon the next day—we slept a bit late; it was still light out when we finally got to bed at about 1 A.M.—the rod jerked violently and then bent nearly double and my father held on for dear life as line screeched from the reel and he said, I'm not kidding, "Christ, I think I've got one!"

We reeled in the other lines as this battle unfolded and I sat there watching my father in the fish fight of his life, a huge smile on his face, and at this moment a son who was now thirty gazed upon the sight of his father sitting beside him in a boat in this marvelous land called Alaska and wondered if he had ever found the beer cans and the condom wrappers I left under the seat of his Mercury when I was in high school, which I thought was an odd thought to have at that moment.

The salmon fought hard in the ice-cold water, tearing off fifty feet of line in seconds and then grudgingly giving some of it back before making another run, and another. My father's smile had turned to a grimace as I offered all the usual words of encouragement fishing partners give each other:

"Keep the rod tip up!"

"He's getting tired!"

"Don't horse him!"

"Your cigar ash has fallen onto your shirt, which is now smoldering!"

After beating out his chest fire, Dad worked the fish closer and closer to the boat and then the guide slid a huge net under the fish and hoisted him from the water, a silver giant of thirty-five pounds or so that posed for a picture with my again-smiling dad and then was released to continue his epic journey to the stream of his birth, where he would find a mate and complete the amazing cycle of a salmon's life. (See *beer cans and condom wrappers* above.)

"Christ, that's a big fish!" my father said. According to my records, this was the 845,987th time in my lifetime that my father had invoked the name of our savior, with 223,346 of those involving his attempted use of a hammer. (Another 1,092 times involved his inability tear a piece of duct tape from the roll.)

We headed south a bit and soon saw a flottill . . . flotila . . . floatyla—a big bunch of boats, perhaps fifty or more, from thirty-footers to inflatable rafts. The bunch of boats was gathered about a half mile offshore, where a river named Deep Creek emptied into the inlet. Deep Creek, we were told, was the birthplace of millions and millions of salmon, and now the tough ones that had survived their long stay in the ocean were coming home.

The incredible salmon are able to smell and identify the fresh water that was their birthplace—detecting even a drop of the fresh water that has been diluted in billions of gallons of salt water, according to biologists. And so they gather at the threshold of their homes and wait until the right moment, when the urge to spawn has become uncontrollable, before suddenly making a mad rush into the river.

This is not entirely unlike the way President Clinton used to wait outside the Intern Break Room in the White House—and I hereby vow not to make another joke about Mr. Clinton unless I think of one.

Alaskan fishing regulations prohibit anglers from getting too close to the mouth of some of the prime spawning rivers—the guide said the no-fishing zone at Deep Creek extended out five hundred yards—to offer the majestic fish a final bit of security on their long journey. So we stayed outside the zone and began the most incredible three hours of fishing imaginable, as giant king salmon slashed at baitfish near the surface in their final feeding frenzy before they entered the river. At that point they would stop eating, begin blindly chasing complete strangers around so they might have sex, and then shrivel up in a pathetic sort of way and slowly die.

(For more information on that subject I suggest the new book *Hugh Hefner: The Autumn Days.*)

Anyway, we hooked ten salmon in those three hours, three of them twenty-pounders and half a dozen that weighed more than thirty pounds. And then I hooked Moby Salmon.

The strike nearly tore the rod from my hands, a stunning, crashing attack that brought me out of my seat and nearly into the frigid water before I steadied myself and watched the line disappearing from the reel. The guide shouted an obscenity and turned the boat and began to give chase. For twenty minutes the battle raged, with the enormous salmon sounding deep beneath us and then suddenly surging away in a display of raw speed and power. He came slowly to the boat in the final minutes of the battle and the guide somehow got most of the fish into the huge net. He was forty-eight inches long. He weighed, the guide said, fifty-five pounds or more.

And even though I hadn't gotten the chance to battle such a monster on a fly rod as I would have liked—I'm sure the battle would have been brief, but I was okay with that—I got to do something just as exciting. I got to let the monstrous king salmon go. I removed the hook, wrapped both hands around his tail, and waited until the oxygen in the cold water had revived him. Then he slammed his massive tail against the side of the boat, sending a wall of water over my father and me, and he was gone.

The fishing seemed less important after that. We caught a few more but nothing to rival the Big One. As the evening sun crept across the sky toward Mount Redoubt and Mount Iliamna, another sight brought a memorable ending to our first day on this marvelous trip.

A man alone in a twelve-foot inflatable raft had hooked a big salmon. And on the calm waters of Cook Inlet, the fish began swimming west, away from the shore, taking the man and his raft

---

RICH TOSCHES

on what I'm sure was an unforgettable trip, moving the craft steadily, relentlessly, toward the middle of the thirty-five-mile-wide inlet. Forty-five minutes after we watched the man hook into the giant, his raft had become just a small red dot on the western horizon.

And through my binoculars I could see that it was still moving.

CHAPTER 27

The Salmon Smoked Me

 I mentioned earlier that I got a few opportunities to unsheathe the Wonder Rod during this trip to Alaska with my father. After determining that it was too dangerous to use in the small boat, a guide said that often, right in front of the lodge, the king salmon would cruise the shoreline in search of the herring that would fill their bellies for the final time.

So I sat on the deck with the guide one night and asked if anyone had ever tried pitching a big streamer fly at them from the shore. He said there had been only one guy in his four years at the lodge who had tried it.

"He'd come back at night looking pretty beat up," Tom the guide said. "He never actually caught one, but he had a helluva time trying."

I wanted a helluva time.

The next evening, after yet another meal that made my own personal ass about three inches wider, I took the Wonder Rod out of its case, which consisted of a five-foot tube of heavy plastic PVC pipe. Before the trip I had loaded 150 yards of twenty-five-pound Dacron backing onto the huge, heavy Pflueger reel. Now I fashioned an eight-foot leader of fifteen-pound test monofilament, tied on a four-inch silver-and-white streamer, and headed down to the beach.

The sun was perched between the volcanoes on the opposite shore, beginning its breathtaking nightly dance of colors. About a hundred feet to my left a pair of bald eagles were squawking over a fish carcass. I sat down on the gravel beach and took it all in, gazing at the eagles for a while and then letting my eyes wander back out to the shimmering water.

Which suddenly exploded.

Some hundred yards down the beach and maybe fifty feet offshore a great burst of water had broken the placid scene. There were seals in the area, and killer whales, too, so at first I didn't know what had caused the commotion. And then a huge silver shape crashed through the surface and came back down with a great splash. Salmon.

I lurched to my feet, moving quickly now toward the splashing, which was coming toward me. I stopped, stripped off as much line as I felt I could throw and double-hauled the line and the giant streamer as far as I could, and waited. When the salmon moved closer I stripped the line back toward me. The water boiled where I knew my fly was skimming under the surface. I stripped again and another monstrous boil surged up behind the fly.

With my heart beating wildly I began stripping line madly, hoping the salmon would be enticed by the sight of the fur-and-feather herring trying to escape. And as I stripped the line a wave came up behind the fly, a wall of water maybe a foot high that began picking up speed. A wave generated by a big salmon as he rushed toward the fly. And then half of his body came out of the water and he struck.

Remember the day when I was kid and was floating a dry fly on the pond at the Nipmuc Rod and Gun Club and the trout came after it and I fell off the dam? Well, that had been two decades earlier, and now, with uncountable hours of experience, I am proud to report that I did NOT fall off a dam.

What I did do was jerk the big streamer away from the monstrous salmon in an adrenaline-laced seizure, stumble backward over a chunk of driftwood, and fall on my back onto the gravel. I looked up in time to see the two eagles, the symbol of America, beating their wings wildly and taking flight to get away from what they probably believed was a seal on crack flopping around on their beach, making the usual sound that a seal on crack makes, a call of nature which sounds like: "Soonoofabitch . . . soonoffaBITCH," as the big mammal struggles to stand up.

The fly line was piled in a heap to my right, the big fly was about fifteen feet farther up the beach, and as you might have guessed, I did not hook that salmon.

Another school of salmon cruised near the beach about forty-five minutes later and I made a few feeble casts, but frankly, my heart wasn't in it anymore. Something told me that when the next salmon made one of those frightening rushes at my fly, I would once again panic, stumble backward, and fall heavily to the ground.

Although, avid fly fisherman that I am, something deep in my soul also told me it would sure be fun to keep trying.

So I thought I'd ask around at the lodge and see if I could borrow a fly-fishing helmet.

The days at Ninilchik Lodge passed much too quickly, even with an extra day that Dad and I got by strategically missing our scheduled flight from Homer to Anchorage. And much too soon the trip had come to an end. It could not have been a better journey.

And I could not have picked a better partner.

CHAPTER 28

Alaska: Even Our Mosquitos Have Pontoons

N ow that I'd made two trips to Alaska, including one with my father, who will always be my number-one fishing partner, I began thinking of a third trip. This one, I thought, should involve the guy I've fished with since childhood, the guy who ate the cow's face near Vail, the guy who now works in a very high-profile law-enforcement capacity in Colorado and would be quite embarrassed to read in this book about a certain someone being arrested in 1972 for having what turned out to be fourteen stolen pumpkins in the trunk of someone's 1965 Ford Mustang.

But I would never do that to him.

Anyway, in 1988 I'd talked to my friend Rob about making a trip to Alaska and he actually frothed at the mouth. The big day finally came in August of 1989. I flew from Los Angeles to Seattle and he flew from Denver to Seattle.

Boy, were our livers tired.

The trip would take us about a hundred miles northwest of Anchorage to the tiny, remote, water-bound village of Skwentna (town motto: "Even Our Mosquitoes Have Pontoons"). I had secured another magazine job to pay for this trip, and the editors allowed me to bring my friend Rob along because of his reputation as an outdoor and wildlife photographer. Though he had never actually, in technical photojournalism terms, "taken a picture while outdoors," I knew he'd be a fast learner and that, more importantly, we'd laugh our asses off for a week in Alaska.

Rob met me as I entered the Seattle-Tacoma airport, and as we walked I knew he was taking this job as photographer seriously because of the way he was mumbling under his breath, "Shiny glass thing is called the lens. Lens points toward the thing you're taking a picture of. Shiny glass thing is the lens . . ."

When we were younger, Rob and I often had what we called "laughing fits"—great, racking uncontrollable bouts of laughter often brought on by nothing. The fits could last thirty seconds or thirty minutes, two kids gasping for air as the fit took on a life of its own, causing its own laughter like a nuclear fission reaction.

Anyway, it was just a childhood thing long ago forgotten as we headed to our next flight with our fly-rod cases tucked under our arms. Soon we'd found our seats on an Alaska Airlines jetliner for the trip to Anchorage, and as we settled in, I mentioned to Rob that perhaps when we got to Alaska we should shoot a grizzly bear in the ass with a tranquilizer dart and then humiliate him by putting things on him such as sunglasses, and then have our pictures taken with him.

But we were adults now, the silliness of youth long abandoned for lives of raising children and paying mortgages. So imagine our surprise when the other passengers began staring at us. Some even moved away.

"And after we drug him we could put his fat ass in a lawn chair . . ."

A flight attendant stopped by to see if we were okay.

"And put a beer in his paw."

"I bet we could get pants on him!!!!"

The howling subsided somewhere over Canada, and we slumped into our seats with sore ribs and watering eyes and stuff coming out of our noses.

We don't know why we laugh this way. We know from years of experience that few other people believe that whatever we are laughing at is funny. We have been criticized for this behavior by friends and family. "For Christ's sake, when are you two gonna grow up?" is the one we hear a lot. (Once I answered that question by saying, "Personally, I believe it will be Thursday"—and we laughed for twenty-six minutes.)

Anyway, I cannot imagine two people who have ever laughed as hard and as long for so many years as Rob and I have.

Unless, of course, you count the two doctors who had treated Monica Lewinsky for carpet burns and then heard President Clinton declare, under oath, "I did not have sex with that woman!"

Somehow the pilot had refrained from joining Rob and me in

this roaring fit, opting instead to continue flying the airplane toward Anchorage. At some point we caught our breath and looked out to see the mountains and glaciers of Alaska. The glaciers were the most impressive. When something is carrying tons and tons of ice and is moving at the speed of one inch every twelve hours, marching relentlessly toward the ocean, you know you are in Alaska. Although it's also possible you are watching Senator Ted Kennedy walking out of the family compound on Cape Cod with another gin and tonic.

The plane began a steep descent into the Anchorage airport, and before we knew it we were in a cab, headed for a nearby airstrip named Merrill Field, where we'd arranged to catch an early evening Cessna flight to Skwentna. Plans had changed, however, and we were told by our pilot that we wouldn't be leaving until the morning. I feared the magazine had conducted a background check and discovered that of the nine photographs Rob had taken in his entire life, six contained the image of his thumb, and that the deal was off.

Turns out it was just a mix-up between the pilot and the lodge, and we'd leave at 7:30 the next morning.

So we got back into the cab and spent that night in Anchorage, at the lovely Voyager Hotel. We had a lovely meal in the evening. Rob had Alaskan halibut, which he said "didn't taste like fish," and I had prime rib, which also didn't taste like fish. We got back to the hotel at about midnight and Rob actually said he'd go to sleep with "visions of salmon dancing in my head."

I had to settle for visions of the seven Moose Head beers I had at dinner dancing in my bladder.

We were out of the hotel by 6:30 A.M. and met our Cessna pilot, Lois, at Merrill Field. Neither Rob nor I had ever flown in a

Cessna before, so we had a lot of questions for Lois. I opened with, "So, Lois, how the hell could you not have figured out that Clark Kent was Superman?"

No, really, we asked about the plane and the flight, learning that we'd be flying in a Cessna Cardinal. (The giveaway was that the safety information cards in the seat pockets were written in Latin, and the plane itself had a big red hat.) We would be traveling at about 140 miles per hour, Lois told us, and the flight to Skwentna would take "just thirty-five minutes, or less." Lois then added that "less" would be the case if the plane crashed before it got to Skwentna. Alaskan pilots joke around like that. Rob and I, who have laughed about such varied topics as shooting bears in the ass with darts and eating a cow's-face burrito, found no humor whatsoever in Lois's comment.

The talk then turned to mosquitoes and Lois laughed. "I start slapping myself when I even think about Skwentna," she said.

By way of comparison, I start slapping myself when I even think about ever getting married again.

Lois continued the comedy routine a few minutes later when she pointed out the left side of the plane and said, "There's the airport." Beneath us, in the dense spruce forest, was a tiny strip of land where the trees had been removed, apparently by beavers. A Skwentna mosquito wouldn't be able to land on it, never mind this Cessna airplane, and Rob and I laughed along with Lois right up until she jerked the steering wheel to the right, dropped the plane out of the sky like a rock, and thumped down on the beaver clearing and said, "Welcome to Skwentna!"

Rob was frightened, speechless, and bug-eyed, but not me. I am much tougher and more rugged than Rob, and so I laughed a long and hearty laugh—and would have laughed even louder and longer, but at this point the urine had soaked through my shorts and pants, and one of my boots.

When the plane rolled to a stop we stumbled out and began removing our bags and fly-rod cases, our minds filled with a million questions. Rob looked at me and posed the first one.

"Did . . . did . . . did we just *crash*?"

Turns out we hadn't, that it was a very typical landing on this patch of dirt that served as the Skwentna airport. We'd been waiting for about ten minutes—Rob looking at his camera and wondering where the film went in, me blowing on my boot to dry it out—when Skwentna Roadhouse lodge owner John Logan showed up, accompanied by two guides, Ray Douglas and T. W.

They had roared through the woods on three all-terrain vehicles carrying three fishermen from Switzerland who had spent the week at the roadhouse and would now be leaving on Lois's plane. We spoke for a few moments with the departing Swiss anglers, not long enough to get to know them but long enough for us to ask them a few critical questions. Rob went with, "So, you guys have those army knives? Can I play with the toothpick and the scissors?"

Being the more intellectual of the two, I apologized for my friend's stupid questions and inquired as to whether they had "brought their own cheese."

The Swiss men climbed into the Cessna then, leaving Rob and me with what I assume was a warm Swiss farewell word ("arsehools") and Ray and T. W. began tossing our stuff onto the four-wheelers. They looked around as they worked, and before we sped off, Ray explained their nervousness.

"Grizzly ate a fisherman two weeks ago, about forty miles from here," he said. "Ate him. They found a sock."

———

Having some expertise in this area, I told the men the bear had probably spit out that one sock because it was, in all likelihood, the sock the man had peed in during the flight to the fishing camp.

I went on to tell them that if the searchers looked hard enough, they'd probably find the man's pants and shorts not too far away.

They just stared at me for a few moments. In the rough bush country of Alaska, admiration and respect must be earned.

I had struck quickly.

CHAPTER 29

Dick Butkus Smells Like a Fish

The Skwentna Roadhouse was charming, a two-story structure made of logs hacked from the nearby forest and painted red, apparently so you can find it easily when a bear is chasing you. Inside we met John's wife, Joyce, who would cook for us for five days and, in this land far from our homes, become somewhat of a mother figure to us. One night, for example, I didn't finish my vegetables and she sent me to bed early despite my whiny, childlike protest. "For chrissakes, Joyce, I'm thirty-six!" were my exact words.

Then she washed my mouth out with soap and said I couldn't keep the puppy.

We gathered that morning at the breakfast table and were told of the great salmon runs that sweep up the Skwentna River and a dozen smaller rivers and streams nearby. Hundreds of thousands of salmon, all of them in a spawning frenzy and eager to attack anything, according to Ray, "bright and flashy and gaudy and cheap looking."

And boy, was he right! On the first day I tied on an eight-by-ten color photograph of Britney Spears and caught 1,456 salmon before noon.

Skwentna, we were also told, is a stop on Alaska's famed Iditarod dogsled race, with thousands of dogs racing up the frozen river and often stopping here for food and a brief rest on their monumental journey. Then, in the spring, as the stunningly cold winter begins to break and the ice begins to thaw, another monumental Alaskan journey takes place: tons of Siberian husky crap washes down the Skwentna River a hundred miles into Anchorage. As I understand it, the fumes from this four-month-old floating dog crap creates gas clouds that float high above the city, creating an eerie nighttime illusion known as the "Northern Lights" or "Aurora Borealis" or "Sasquatch."

Our fishing journey would begin by traveling up the Skwentna River, a magical place of pools and eddies and fast-moving currents, a special river where, according to native Alaskan legend, *salmas tas dogj paap* ("the salmon taste like dog poop").

We piled onto a four-wheeler for the short trip from the roadhouse to the river and then found ourselves in a sixteen-foot boat, screaming across the raging Skwentna River, the boat powered by a Yamaha-brand jet outboard motor as Ray expertly guided the craft between gigantic logs and floating trees torn from the shore by the surging river. The Skwenta was full of salmon, he told us, but the volume of heavy, brown water roaring down the two-hundred-foot-wide river made it unfishable. So we'd use the Skwentna as our highway, traveling to dozens of tributaries where the water flowed clear and cold.

The temperature was about 42 degrees that morning, and combined with the speed of the boat, this created a pleasant windchill factor I estimated at 1,786 degrees below zero—using a complicated mathematical formula that includes temperature, wind speed, humidity, and how many minutes go by before you can no longer feel your testicles.

As we zoomed along I sat in the front of the boat, bravely serving as a windbreak for my friend Rob, who huddled behind me in the middle seat deftly ducking the snot-cicles that were breaking off the end of my nose and hurtling back toward him.

After about half an hour Ray slowed the Hypothermia Express and slid the boat into a seventy-five-foot-wide river that emptied into the Skwentna. Soon, after determining that at least one of my testicles was still in the boat, I picked up my fly rod and began casting a bright orange streamer toward the bank.

When a trout sips a dry fly floating on a placid stream or creek, it is a wonderful thing, the gentle rise of the fish as the fly disappears in a small splash. It speaks of the serenity and peace that we all long for in this ever-changing world of ours. When, on the other hand, a salmon hits a fly, it's like Hall of Fame Chicago Bears' linebacker Dick Butkus crashing into you, except in this case Dick Butkus is silver, smells like a fish, and has been interrupted while trying to have sex in the gravel at the bottom of a river—which I'm sure did not actually happen to Mr. Butkus more than a couple of times in his entire NFL career.

Anyway, that's what it was like when the first silver salmon struck on the first day, a thud that jolted my arm and ran all the way up to the bones of my shoulder blades or "spatulas." The spot was a tributary of the Skwentna River, a place called Eight-Mile Creek that was perhaps twenty feet wide at the point where our guide, Ray, had eased the big flat-bottomed boat. The fly was a bright orange streamer, and as I stripped it slowly back toward the boat, the salmon rushed at it from twenty-five feet away. And in the clear water I reacted the way I always do in these situations: I made a pathetic, whining, sissy sound and tried to pull the fly away from the rushing fish.

This time, however, even my bad habit was no match for the speed of the fish, and he crashed into it with all the fury of Richard Simmons attacking a pie when no one is looking. I set the hook and the fish streaked away and the rod nearly came out of my hand. Ray, who had seen this sight perhaps a thousand times in his years in Alaska, remained eerily calm as he lurched to feet and shouted "Keee-rist almighty!" and scrambled for the net.

About fifteen minutes later we had our first salmon in the boat. Ray unhooked the fly and lowered the net back into the stream, and the fish, thirty-two inches long and perhaps fifteen pounds of silver power, exploded from it, racing back to the gravel bottom, where he would, as hundreds of generations of spawning salmon before him had done, get lucky. Then he would smoke a cigarette before being asked to leave, although I might be confusing him with me.

I collapsed back onto the seat of the boat, nearly crushing the three sack lunches Ray had prepared for us earlier that morning—

each bag containing a huge, manly sandwich made of a delicious native meat they called *slosledpooch,* which I later learned means "slow sled dog."

As I sat there trying to catch my breath, I noticed a large metal plate welded to the bottom of the boat, covering what might have been a big hole. I asked Ray about this.

"Couple years ago, about a mile up this creek, a grizzly came out of the bushes and stood up," he said. "I carried a .357 magnum and the son of a bitch kept coming, like he was going to get into the boat with us. So I stood up in the boat and took out the gun to fire a shot in the air to scare him. I was pretty nervous. And I accidentally shot a hole in the bottom of the boat. We almost drowned.

"I don't carry guns anymore when I'm fishing."

This was, as you might imagine, a comforting thought, reminding Rob and me of the National Rifle Association's famous saying: "Guns don't kill people. Grizzly bears kill people by standing up and making the people pee in their trousers and then shoot a hole in their boat."

For the rest of the trip we found great peace knowing that while we were in the capable hands of superb guide Ray Douglas, there would be no tragic firearm accidents. The trade-off, of course, was that it remained possible there would be a tragic having-your-ass-chewed-by-a-grizzly-bear accident, with our guide valiantly trying to save his clients by repeatedly striking the thousand-pound bear on the head with a net.

Or a *slosledpooch* sandwich.

Eight-Mile Creek was filled with salmon on this day, thousands of fish that had already made a brutal journey of some sixty miles up the Skwentna River from the Gulf of Alaska and had now found their birth stream by using a miraculous sense of smell honed by thousands and thousands of years of instinct. Although a few of them, the so-called yuppy salmon, had used handheld GPS locators. They were generally shunned by the rest of the school.

Rob and I stood in the boat and peered into the clear water and shouted with excitement as the salmon swam by, sometimes alone, sometimes in small "packs" or "herds"—their powerful tails propelling them with lightning speed into the current. I would make a second cast and hook another salmon a moment later, this one leaping clear of the water and landing with a splash as Rob stood behind me, his shaking hands trying to tie a fly to his leader as he shouted encouragement to his longtime friend, encouragement that sounded like "You bastard!"

Ray had netted this second fish and returned it to the water before my slow friend was ready to make his first cast. He brought the fly back with slow twitches, mostly because his hands were still shaking, and just ten feet from the boat a big silver charged and struck and the line began peeling from his reel. Rob, who swears more than any person on earth, was only able to shout three "holy shits" and one "sonofabitch" before the fish rushed back toward him. The line slackened and the salmon shook the fly free from its mouth.

It is at these times when friendship is most important, when a man needs to know that despite a bit of bad luck he is still admired and appreciated by the man standing next to him in the boat, that a friendship born some thirty years earlier is still alive and well.

So I shouted, "What a loser!" and made my third cast, hooking yet another salmon and bringing him to the net as my friend looked on in admiration, turning away only briefly to open my sack lunch and spit into the bag.

Eventually, Rob hooked another salmon and battled it skillfully. Near the boat it jumped from the water, its silver sides flashing in the Alaska sun before Ray slid the net under it and Rob pumped his fist in celebration. I had videotaped the entire battle, putting aside my own fly rod when Rob had set the hook and capturing my friend's battle with the strong fish so that someday his children could sit in the living room with their father and watch as their hero fought a large salmon in the Alaska wilderness, their hearts filled with pride and wonder as they asked, "Dad, what does 'son of a bitch big bastard goddammit' mean?"

We caught fifteen more silver salmon, magnificent fish between eight and eighteen pounds, fish that had two grown men mumbling and stammering and exchanging excited glances just as they did decades earlier—first when they hooked bass and bluegills in the small ponds of Massachusetts and in later years when a police officer opened the trunk of a Mustang and asked, "Where'd you get all the pumpkins?"

Our first fishing day in Alaska had been a stunning one, filled with joy and laughter and excitement and breathtaking battles with tremendous fish. We were exhausted, beaten into a happy fatigue by the drama.

It was noon.

Ray turned the boat down Eight-Mile Creek and back into the raging Skwentna River. We regrouped at the roadhouse for a few hours, sitting on the porch in the warm rays of the sun and babbling about the morning we'd had as we tried to digest the dog sandwiches we'd eaten.

Note: I am making up the dog sandwiches stuff. However, I am not making up any of the following: The meat in the sandwiches was, I swear, moose! It was my first-ever moose sandwich and it was good.

Then, after lunch, I lowered my head and attacked a sled dog and was shot to death by roadhouse owner John, who then mounted my head over his fireplace.

CHAPTER 30

Rob Gets to Drive the Boat

After lunch and a nap Ray said it was time to go to his cabin, which was not in what you'd call an urban setting, like the house owned by my friends Doug and Caryn in the Los Angeles area. Their house was in the seaside town of Hermosa Beach. On Super Bowl Sunday in 1982, we gathered there to watch the big football game, which pitted the Miami Dolphins against the Brooklyn Dodgers, I think. We drank a lot that day.

Anyway, just before kickoff I plopped my large behind into a chair in their living room. Suddenly the sound of gushing water hit my ears. It sounded as if a pipe had broken. I was alarmed. Doug stuffed another handful of salsa into his mouth and just sat there. I couldn't believe he wasn't dashing madly around the house searching for duct tape like a normal guy. Finally, I got out of my chair and said, "Doug! I think a pipe broke. Don't you hear that water?"

He stopped chewing for a moment, listened, and then announced, "It's the guy next door. He's peeing."

Doug's house was separated from the neighbor's house by a distance I would estimate to be, oh, two feet. As I was sitting there, beside an open window—January in L.A. can bring bone-chilling temperatures such as sixty-eight degrees—what I was listening to was not a broken pipe. It was, indeed, his next door neighbor urinating in his own bathroom, into, hopefully, the toilet, which was twenty-four inches from the window in Doug's house.

So I settled back into my chair to enjoy the Super Bowl, hoping for a close, exciting game in which the Dolphins and Dan Marino would triumph and the guy next door would not accidentally pee on me.

By way of contrast, if you sat in Ray Douglas's home and heard the loud sound of urinating outside the window, it would not be his next-door neighbor. It would a moose. Or a raccoon with a healthy prostate gland.

We climbed back into the Skwentna Roadhouse jet boat and set off on the river again, roaring along for one hour at a speed of twenty miles per hour. How far had we traveled?

(a) 20 miles
(b) The train from Chicago.

———

RICH TOSCHES

(c) Trains A and B would meet in Peoria.

(d) Go on with the damn fly-fishing book, you Attention Deficit Disorder poster boy!

The correct answer is (d), of course, and soon Ray had turned the boat into an area called Donkey Slew. This was either a shallow swampy lagoon or an odd-looking animal created when famous racehorse Seattle Slew screwed a donkey.

Anyway, we raced through Donkey Slew and then up Donkey Creek toward Ray's cabin. Along the way we saw an interesting thing: a black bear crashed into the narrow, ten-foot-wide creek about a hundred feet ahead of us, looked at us briefly, and then crashed through the willows and ran away. I was glad to have seen such a spectacular show of nature. I was also glad I'd brought forty-five pairs of underwear on this trip because when we got back to the roadhouse I was going to need at least one clean pair.

I failed to mention earlier that one week prior to the Alaska trip I had sprained an ankle playing softball. I was wearing a soft cast and was limping badly throughout the adventure. So when this brief confrontation took place with the black bear—which are, they say, less dangerous than a grizzly bear, although much more dangerous than, say, a chipmunk—my childhood friend Rob reminded me of one important thing: If we should be attacked by any sort of bear, he and Ray would have nothing but nice thoughts about me as they ran away and left me to be eaten.

After pausing to let the bear go on his way, Ray cranked up the jet boat again and we roared past the spot where the large beast had trampled small trees along the creek and we continued upstream for another hour or so. Eventually the creek widened and we skimmed over a gravel bar and onto a lake, which was not, surprisingly, named Donkey Lake. Several hundred yards up Not Donkey Lake, Ray rammed the bow of the boat into the shore and said, "We're here!"

I was crying and refused to get out of the boat. Eventually, however, they coaxed me out and we strolled—well, they strolled; I limped—a mile and a half up a trail. And somehow found ourselves at Ray's home, which he and his wife built from cutting down trees. It took them three years to build the sixteen-by-sixteen cabin, where they would raise Raymond Jr. and Holly— perhaps the only two kids in America who believe Nintendo is an intestinal disorder you get from drinking from a stream that a bear has pooped in.

The scene was surreal. We had flown a hundred miles from Anchorage into the Alaskan bush. Then we had traveled some forty miles via boat up a big river, through a slew, up another creek, and halfway down a lake with no real name before staggering for another hour up a steep forest trail. And someone lived here!

I was speechless, in part because of the realization of just how far we were from any semblance of civilization, but also because my bad ankle had now swelled up to the size of a watermelon.

And then Ray told us a story:

As they were building the cabin, on forty acres of wilderness land the state of Alaska had given them, they looked down from their hillside and noticed one day that across the huge lake was a tiny speck on the opposite shoreline: another cabin. It was, they figured, about a ten-mile walk around the lake to get there and they didn't have any extra time or energy, so they never made the trip. But one summer day an old man approached them as they sawed logs, Ray said. They had seen him walking along the opposite shoreline in a bright red coat earlier in the day, and now he appeared from the forest.

They were thrilled to have some company and couldn't wait to sit down with him and talk.

The old man, perhaps seventy, Ray said, did all the talking.

"You've got the whole goddamn state of Alaska," he told Ray and his wife, "and you gotta come build your cabin *right on top of mine?*"

And then the old man turned and walked back into the forest toward his own cabin. Ray and his wife never saw him again. About a year later, Ray said, he trekked over to the old man's cabin and found it abandoned. The old man, clearly sensing that the area was about to become a subdivision and that he'd be listening to his neighbors peeing during the Super Bowl, had packed up all of his belongings and left. Ray said he'd probably gone deeper into the forest and built another cabin, away from all the hustle and bustle.

In this setting, fifteen-year-old Ray Douglas, Jr. and his sister, Holly, sixteen, seemed stunningly happy. At the Skwentna High School—she stayed with friends in the village during the week—Holly was ranked number one in her senior class. Nobody was number two. She was the only member of the senior class—making it pretty hard to blow a spitball at the teacher and then look innocent. On the plus side, Holly had clearly locked up the Most Likely to Succeed award.

Seriously, Holly was just like any sixteen-year-old American girl, except for little things, such as having once shot a moose through her front door. She and Ray Jr. were delightful and never once said, "Uh, like, hello, like, you know?" like most teenagers. Rob and I liked them a lot.

———

ZIPPING MY FLY

199

And Ray's wife was terrific, too, exuding that fierce, independent spirit that comes from having to stoop over to pick her husband's underwear up off the floor—underwear that she had lovingly made for him out of a snowshoe-hare pelt.

Which explained why whenever Ray would scratch himself, his nose began to twitch.

Soon, all of us headed down the trail—including me, who Ray Jr. had given the proud native nickname *berbaet* ("bear bait")—and we climbed into the boat for the wild and furious ride back to Skwentna, where the Douglas family would pick up some supplies before heading back the next day to their little paradise in the Alaskan woods.

Along the way we came upon another fishing boat that had run aground on a sandbar. We climbed out and spent about an hour—to use the technical waterway navigational term—"unsticking it" and sending our fellow anglers on their way.

"Up here you stop and help," Ray said. "Otherwise people die."

We had another great dinner at the roadhouse that night. Salmon and a pot roast. We had kept one fish from our first day on Eight-Mile Creek, a seven- or eight-pound fish that would serve the entire gang of guides, along with Joyce and John. I don't eat fish. As a boy in New England, I wouldn't even eat seafood. My father and brother ate clams all summer, but I couldn't fathom the idea of eating any creature that made its home between two ashtrays. So everyone thought I was strange. Not so much because of the seafood thing. Mostly because I liked to wear lipstick.

Just kidding.

Rob and I stayed up until after midnight talking about this incredible experience. At 1:00 A.M., John shut off the generator and the lights went out. We settled into our beds, which John had made from the trees of the forest. The light from the full moon shone . . . shined . . . shinyed . . . came through our window, and because I was now a grown-up, I only made hand shadows on the bedroom wall for about twenty minutes instead of three hours like I did when I was in my late twenties. The morning would bring us twenty-five miles up the neighboring Yentna River, which flows out of Denali National Park, and up a tributary called the Talachilitna ("I think we are lost").

It would turn out to be even better than our first day.

We finally went to sleep with visions of huge salmon on fly rods dancing in our heads.

Although Rob kept saying it looked like a wolf and said he'd kick my ass if I didn't stop making the damn hand shadows.

By 9 A.M. we'd settled into our usual positions in the boat. Ray fired up the jet outboard and we were off, roaring up the Yenta River at 30 mph. Without slowing, Ray shouted that he had to untangle some line and switched seats with Rob, who was now piloting the boat. Here is an actual entry from Rob's journal, a diligent and detailed account of our trip that I borrowed for this book. My own journal was, uh, eaten by the big, hairy half-man, half-monster that roams these north woods: "Aurora Borealis."

Anyway, here's Rob's account of what was clearly the most exciting moment of the entire trip:

> We're at full speed/Ray says 30 mph/I'm driving. I think I feel Ray grab the controls again, so I let go.

Here's my account of what happened next:

JESUSCHRIST OHMYGOD GRAB THE MOTOR OH DEAR GOD AAAAHHH-HHHHH!!!!!!

Ray had NOT, in fact, grabbed the outboard throttle handle back from Rob, who was apparently delirious. So when Rob released the throttle handle, the outboard pivoted all the way to the left, sending the craft into a 30-mph snap turn to the right and directly toward the riverbank, which was roughly one inch away. Rob had actually stood up to return to his seat when he'd felt "Ray grab the controls" and was now hanging over the edge, perilously close to a dive into the thirty-five-degree raging river in the out-of-control boat.

Ray leaped from his seat, lunged at the outboard motor as we missed the shoreline by one-one-hundredth of an inch or less, and got us headed back up the river.

"Keeee-rist!" Ray said. "What the hell happened?"

Rob babbled about "feeling" someone grab the controls and about wolf shadows on the bedroom wall and some other shit, and Ray told us how close we came to dying.

I sat in the bow, unflinching, staring bravely ahead, lost in my own thoughts. These thoughts centered around how forty-five pairs of underwear didn't seem to be nearly enough for a trip like this. About twenty minutes later, as we approached the Talachilitna and I had calmed down enough to be able to let out a series of shrill screams, we eased into the most awe-inspiring scene I'd ever witnessed. The tributary was clear, about a hundred feet wide, and as it flowed into the Yentna, great billowing clouds of mist rose from the surface and hung just above the river. The stunning Alaska range loomed in the background, a dense spruce forest crept up to the banks, the rays of the sun were filtered through the misty air, and amid it all, enormous salmon seemed to be flying from the river—giants of twenty and thirty pounds, hanging for a moment in the pristine air before smacking back down onto the water with a loud *crack*.

Just as Aldo Leopold and John Muir and John Audubon before me, I became entranced by the vision stretching before me and summoned up the eloquence only such majestic scenes can inspire, declaring, in a loud and emotional voice: "Hooolllly shit!"

Rob: "Holy shit is right! Look at this $%^&*# place!"

The salmon came at our flies then in a frantic way, thumping the streamers with a vengeance that spoke directly to their unhappiness at being kept from having sex. We caught a dozen or so, and lost a few that were, simply, too big and too strong to handle on our six- and seven-weight fly rods. We didn't much care. It was one of the few times in my three decades of fly-fishing that the scenery defeated the actual fishing and earned a place in my permanent, unending memory—a day so vivid that nothing could ever erase the images.

Did I mention the part about Rob letting go of the $%^&*# outboard throttle and nearly killing everyone?

That night, Rob walked from the roadhouse and sat among the nineteen sled dogs that were being kept and trained on John's property. In his journal he wrote: "I really felt like I was in Alaska when I was sitting with those dogs. What a great feeling!"

(In their journal, the dogs wrote: "Visited this evening by the knucklehead who 'felt' someone else grab the outboard motor throttle, causing him to let go. What a dipshit!")

The next day we were met at the breakfast table by the other guide, who went by T. W. or just plain T, (who would take us out today because, well, I think because after two days with us Ray had an appointment with a psychiatrist.)

T, who was a funny guy, took us back up the Yentna River to a tributary called Johnson Creek. The highlight of the day came when I hooked what I believe was either a king salmon or a seal on methamphetamines. I set the hook and within seconds was down to the backing on the reel. Within thirty seconds the creature had all my fly line and the backing stripped from the reel. I grabbed the final three feet, wrapped it around my hand, and was dragged about five feet across the gravel before I felt the sixteen-pound test leader pop some 150 yards downstream.

T, who had watched the whole thing with a smile on his face, said, "Did someone have a bite?"

Another night of good food, great stories, and a spectacular hand-shadow show followed. It would be our last night in Alaska.

The final day of fishing would be the best.

CHAPTER 31

The Meowing Sissy Boy

T had us back in the boat at 9 A.M. We believe T is insane. A good kind of insane. He often laughs for no apparent reason, laughs harder when something is the least bit funny, and laughs so hard stuff comes out his nose at the real funny stuff. Rob and I liked him.

It rained hard as we raced a mile down the Skwentna River and turned up the Yentna River. It was about sixty-five degrees and the rain felt good. We're headed back to Johnson Creek. I am holding a grudge against whatever the hell it was that I'd hooked the day before.

———

Rob had watched my brief, one-sided battle with that fish and began this day with a heavy spinning rod. Being an avid fly angler, I looked down my nose at him. He made his first cast and his heavy lure snagged the bottom. He gave a mighty tug and the spinning rod snapped, the top two feet dangling like a . . . well, like something that dangles.

God is a fly fisherman.

Today, T says we should try drifting egg-pattern flies near the bottom in hopes of enticing the giant salmon that are surging out of the Yentna River and into Johnson Creek. Unlike the streamer fly-fishing we'd been doing, this approach involves making long casts upstream and then watching the floating fly line to detect a strike.

Because I've nymph-fished for years in this manner, watching the indicator for the slightest twitch that might suggest the subtle strike of a trout, I was able to detect my first strike quite easily.

This was because the fly line suddenly straightened out and made a loud hissing sound as it sliced through the water. I set the hook and hung on as a monstrous salmon headed, it seemed, back toward the ocean. But this time I applied heavy pressure from the start of the fight and turned the fish, which now ran upstream and passed within ten feet of my legs. It was gigantic. I made a noise that sounded like "Eeeeiiiiiyip!" as the fish, some forty inches long, I thought, streaked past.

T said, "Does someone have another bite?" I said, "Bite ME!" and we all laughed.

Twenty minutes later I slid the fish onto the gravel bar, a massive king salmon that stretched out at forty-three inches and weighed twenty-five pounds or so. I released the big male, and as I held him by the tail in the river, he thanked me by spraying me with quite a bit of white, milky fish semen.

———

RICH TOSCHES

Quite frankly, a handshake or even a nod would have been enough thanks.

For three hours Rob and I and our new friend T stood in the clear waters of Johnson Creek as salmon jumped all around us. Rob's journal says: "Rich and I were about thirty feet apart and a huge salmon began jumping right between us. Then it headed straight at me and came completely out of the water within five feet of me! It scared me a little bit. I thought he might hit me! He didn't, but his splash soaked me. Rich laughed as I started swearing at the fish."

The swearing, however, had hardly begun.

After we took a lunch break—T started a driftwood fire on the gravel bar and cooked cheeseburgers—we waded back into Johnson Creek for our final few hours of fishing. I began catching a big salmon on every cast, the powerful fish attacking the egg-pattern fly along the bottom.

Then, standing twenty feet downstream of me, Rob sets the hook and his reel begins screeching. I turn just in time to see him start hopping up and down in the river, obscenities echoing off the Alaska range. As the monstrous salmon began a roaring downstream run, Rob had reached awkwardly for his fly reel to slow the fish and the handle, which was going around at roughly 467,000 rpm, slammed into his right, or nose-picking, hand.

The nail on his middle finger was torn completely off. The nail on his thumb was smashed and purple. T and I raced over and did what we could. That's right, we make a $10 bet, with me insisting the salmon will actually kill my childhood friend in the next five minutes. A $5 side bet says the salmon will then eat Rob.

Fifteen minutes later I lose the bet, narrowly, as the fish appears to feel sorry for Rob and comes to the net.

From Rob's journal: "My hand hurts but it doesn't matter. I've learned to keep my fingers out of the way."

He was thirty-nine years old at the time. I was just glad I hadn't done anything that stupid.

My big fish came about half an hour later, a salmon as powerful as the previous day's giant slamming the fly and heading downstream. The reel screamed and the handle whirred around like the propeller on my beanie, and then the fish turned suddenly into an even heavier current, where Johnson Creek emptied into the raging Yentna. A moment later the salmon raced to the right and sulked in the shallow riffles far, far away.

T was just a blur then as he sprinted past me in his hip boots, net in hand, racing toward the fish. About a hundred yards downstream he waded into the heavier water, plunged the net into the river, and pulled it back out with my fish in it. It was a king of about twenty-six pounds, he figured. He pumped a fist in the air, I did the same, and he released the giant in a calm stretch of water where it could catch its breath.

We fished late into the afternoon and then into the evening, the sun still high in the blue Alaskan sky but our wristwatches telling us that, well, telling me that Mickey's little hand was on the eight and his big hand was on the six, so I think it was about five minutes past noon.

We got back to the roadhouse late that night. Joyce helped me wash out a deep gash on my right index finger and bandage it up. Rob said I had actually stuck the finger into my reel, between the frame and the spool, during the last fight with the big salmon. He said the cut bled for twenty minutes and turned the edge of the river red and left my shirt spattered with blood and that I actually made a sissylike meowing sound like a hungry kitten.

———

RICH TOSCHES

Joyce worked on the cut as I looked down at my shirt, which appeared to be covered with ketchup, probably from the lunchtime cheeseburgers. And as the sun faded over the Alaska range on the final night of one helluva fishing trip, my dear friend finished telling his tall tale ("The Big Salmon and the Meowing Sissy Boy," he called it) and I just laughed.

Stuck my finger into my reel. Right. Like I'm some kind of idiot.

As Joyce finished wrapping my finger in about fifteen feet of gauze and tape, I wondered how Rob comes up with stuff like that.

CHAPTER 32

So That's What Trouties Look Like

As a man who has been blessed with great skill in the area of fly-fishing, I began looking early for the telltale signs that my offspring had, perhaps, inherited this remarkable trait—a special gene that would allow them to spot a rising trout, select just the right fly, move quietly into position, and snag a giant willow shrub behind them on the $%^&*@ bank.

Maggie came first, a large bundle of joy born on Thanksgiving Day in 1985. I can still see the look on the doctor's face as the miracle of childbirth was completed and I grabbed her chubby little leg and shouted, "Ohhhhh, I got the drumstick!"

I didn't introduce Maggie to fishing right away, of course. She was just a baby and would need time to grow and develop before stepping into this world of rivers and streams and wild trout and the dangers associated with this sort of thing. So I waited until she was three.

Our first trip together brought us five hours north of Los Angeles, along the Owens River, where she would catch the pet grasshoppers and hand them to her daddy for safekeeping. But then it was time for bigger things, so it was on to the eastern edges of Yosemite National Park, to a place called June Lake, nestled high in the Sierras. Because she was just three, I knew I could not spend nights in the great outdoors the way I usually did—curled up in the fetal position on the cold ground near a smoldering fire made of wet wood, a pine branch my blanket and an empty bottle of Jack Daniel's my pillow.

No, on her first trip the princess would need a tent and a sleeping bag. So on that April day I set up camp just like a Boy Scout, capturing the essence of scouting later in the afternoon by accidentally shooting an adult in the eye with a BB gun.

We would fish in the morning, but now it was time for sleep. So we crawled into the tent, snuggled into our sleeping bags, and listened as two owls serenaded us. It was a special time, that first night in the wild with my princess. And we talked.

"Da-da," little Maggie asked. "Why do owls say 'who'?"

"What?"

" 'Who.' Owls say 'who.' Why?"

"When?"

"Now, da-da. Why 'who'?"

"Why who *what?*"

"Owls who. Why?"

"Uh, I think I hear a bear outside, Maggie! Bears eat little girls if they hear them talking."

Today, Maggie is sixteen. And sometimes I regret having told her that little fib about the bears. Never is this more true than when she walks into the room while I'm watching my favorite TV show. As soon as she sees Yogi or his pal, Boo-Boo, she begins shaking and screaming until I can wrestle her to the floor and give her the medication.

I don't blame her, of course.

I blame those $%^&* owls.

Another memorable thing happened that same night. It took place long after the owls had suddenly shut up, almost as though someone had lurched out of a tent and thrown a Jack Daniel's bottle high up into the tree at them and would then pick the bottle up the next morning because I, I mean they, didn't want to be known as a litterbug.

Anyway, around midnight it began to snow.

It was a heavy, driving snow that quickly built up on our tent as Maggie slept in her sleeping bag. I wondered if the tent might collapse, leaving a father and his three-year-old daughter to stagger around in the wilderness until we could find a member of the Donner Party who might still be wandering around in these California forests and be willing to share his leg of Al with us.

Then I dozed off to sleep, only to be awakened a few hours later by the loud screaming of a child. It turned out to be Maggie, who had, in her sleep, climbed out of the sleeping bag and then climbed back in—headfirst.

In the near-total darkness I reached for where her head had

been, but found only two small feet. I climbed out of my own sleeping bag, found her head by beating around the tent with my hand until something shouted "Ouch!" and then somehow dragged her back out. She was crying, so I held her for a while and told her what had happened. Then she laughed, we climbed into the sleeping bags feet first, and slept until morning as the snow kept coming down.

In the morning it was twenty-five degrees outside, so I packed up all the camping gear and rented a nice warm cabin for the next three days.

During one of those days, Maggie caught her first trout.

She squealed.

(It was a different squeal from the one she made a dozen years later, when her first boyfriend came to the door and I gave him a little advice: "I have a shotgun, a shovel, and three acres out back. Have her home before ten.")

After another day or two on that first fishing expedition in which I showed her how Daddy fly-fishes ("Da-da, how come you never catch any fishies?") we headed for home, stopping along the way at the Lone Pine trout hatchery near Mount Whitney. We fed the trout ("So that's what trouties look like!") and then Maggie sat on the grass, pulled out a piece of paper and her crayons, and drew a map showing how we would get out of the hatchery and make our way back to Los Angeles.

She believed the map was our only hope of finding our way home, and I, of course, went along with the whole thing, asking her all the way back to L.A. where I should turn and which road we should take next.

We laughed the entire way, a father and his little girl enjoying a precious day together.

———

RICH TOSCHES

I didn't stop laughing until we saw the sign that read WELCOME
TO EUGENE, OREGON.

Nick came along next, in 1989, the cutest little guy you could
ever imagine. Nick greeted me in the hospital delivery room—I
am not kidding about this—by peeing directly into my eye within
forty-five seconds of his birth. I was holding him at the moment
the fountain erupted, and after I regained my composure, I smiled
an awkward smile and then hugged my son.

You know, right after I'd picked him up off the floor and kissed
the big lump on his head. The doctor said the little guy probably
traveled about seven feet across the room and I had to take his
word for it because I had staggered out into the hallway shouting,
"I'm blind! I'm blind!"

Three years later Nick and Maggie and I went back to June
Lake, where Nick made his fishing debut. I rigged a fly behind
a plastic bubble and would cast it far out onto the lake for him
and let him reel it back in. And on this very day, he caught a
trout!

But more importantly, it was during that outing that little Nick,
who had only known the congestion and urban ways of Los Angeles, learned to pee in the woods instead of in a toilet or my eye.

The discovery thrilled him and he spent endless hours that
week wandering around the lake and nearby streams, urinating
like there was no tomorrow. Or if there was a tomorrow, it was
going to be yellow and wet. Wherever he was when the urge
came, he'd drop his little tiny trousers and pee and laugh.

But all too soon the trip ended and we found ourselves back in
L.A. I dropped Nick off at his preschool on Monday morning and
returned around 2 P.M.

"Uh, Mr. Tosches, we need to talk," said his teacher, Miss Shelley. "Nicholas peed in the sandbox today while the other children were playing in it."

As I understand it, the little guy nearly filled the moat in someone's sand castle.

"Do you have any idea why he'd do a thing like that?" a highly concerned Miss Shelley asked.

Knowing the bond between a parent and teacher is based on trust, I told her the truth: His evil sister had bet him $5 he wouldn't urinate in the sandbox.

I told Miss Shelley I'd have a stern talk with both of them over this incident.

Back home, I sat Nick down and explained that he couldn't pee outside anymore, that we were back in civilization now and all bathroom functions would once again have to take place in a bathroom, not on someone's sand castle.

He hugged me and said Okay. Then he added, "Daddy, I think I washed out the drawbridge."

I don't think I have to tell you how proud I was.

Three years later the third and final addition arrived. John was the fearless one, the one I could not scare by leaping out from under the kitchen table and shouting "Boo!"—as I had done with Maggie and Nick and as my father had done to me. (He stopped doing that when I was thirty-four because, frankly, it had just become stupid. And, of course, because Dad was then in his sixties and would sometimes get tangled up under one of the chairs and we'd have to help him out.)

Anyway, by the time John turned one, we had moved to Colorado and the fishing trips were now more frequent. He'd caught his first trout before he was three and seemed to love this outdoor life. Once, on a blustery winter day high in the Rockies, I brought

---

the kids onto the Antero Reservoir and introduced them to ice fishing, which is sometimes what we do as we await the return of spring and the fantastic fly-fishing it brings.

I have an ice-fishing hut, a black tentlike structure that stays toasty warm inside as you stare through the hole in the ice waiting for a trout to bite. I had been waiting like that for five winters. Once, I thought I saw a trout swim by, but it turned out to be my own foot twitching after my leg had fallen asleep.

So one day I left John and Nick inside the warm ice-fishing shelter and told them I'd be back in a minute. I paused outside for a while, but they apparently thought I had walked away. I know this because suddenly, in a voice that ripped through the tent and echoed off the mountains, John, who was four at the time, shouted (I am not kidding about this):

"HOLY SHIT!"

I shouted, "Hey!"

John shouted, "Uh-oh!"

That kind of language is not what you want a four-year-old using, and so I unzipped the ice hut to deliver quite a lecture on the use of foul language. Inside, I saw little John standing up, his ice-fishing rod doubled over, engaged in a death struggle with some type of monster lurking beneath the ice. So I yelled, "Holy shit!" and began coaching him, screaming at him to relax and take it easy and not to horse the fish or he'd break the line.

Suddenly the head of the largest rainbow trout I'd ever seen in my life appeared down inside the hole. I plunged my entire arm into the frigid water and slowly eased the giant through the ice and onto the floor of the hut.

I took a photo of John holding the monster of some twenty-six inches, then we slipped the fish back into the water.

A few moments later John and I talked about swearing and how it's not okay and that I didn't want him to use that kind of language anymore—unless he hooked a huge trout like he'd just done and then it was okay as long as, like, he wasn't fishing with a priest or anything.

I wanted Nick to hear this little talk, too, but he was outside.

Peeing his initials into the snow.

Maggie, Nick, and John are my all-time favorite fishing companions.

CHAPTER 33

The Children and the Elk Droppings

I bought my kids their own fly rods and waders in 1998. I told them how their grandpa had bought me my own fly rod when I was twelve. John looked puzzled and then asked, "Did they have trout back then?" I told him we did, but often, as we reeled them in, gigantic screeching pterodactyls would swoop down from the ash-filled sky, which is how the sky was back then when the earth was still forming, and grab the fish away from us.

Today, whenever John hooks a trout he quickly looks up at the sky. Last summer, as he battled a trout on the Taylor River, I snuck up behind him and let out a loud, prehistoric-sounding *screech,* which made his brother, Nick, pee all over his own boots. Maggie dove headfirst into her sleeping bag.

Our first outing with the new fly rods came on Pikes Peak, the stunningly beautiful mountain that rises out of Colorado Springs, Colorado. We drove about halfway to the summit and then hiked about a mile, cutting off a trail and heading down to North Catamount Reservoir, with someone pausing briefly to scoop up a handful of dried elk pellets and toss them at someone else. When we reached the shoreline I washed my hands in the water and we continued around the reservoir to a secluded spot where big, cruising cutthroat rose steadily amid a hatch of small caddis flies. I rigged up their fly rods and we began the long, slow process of learning the basics of casting, something that took me nearly five years of relentless practice.

They had it down in about fourteen minutes, throwing tight loops thirty feet out onto the water and then waiting for the trout to come. And they did, slashing at the artificial caddis in big swirls. This is where fly-fishing gets tough, I told them, when the fish rise and your heart pounds and invariably you yank the fly away before the fish actually has it because the fish are so smart.

"This one isn't!" said Maggie, her fly rod bent as she slowly backed away from the water and eased a fifteen-inch trout gently onto the gravel.

"Wow, that's great, honey! Way to go. Sometimes the fish just hit so hard it's easy to hook them. I'm so proud of you. And if you miss a few, don't feel bad."

She hooked the next five trout that rose to her fly, hesitating perfectly at the strike and then setting the hook just as her dad learned to do after only twenty-five years of fly-fishing.

———

RICH TOSCHES

Nick, however, had his dad's yippy nerves. After watching him set the hook too early on his first two strikes, I told him to count "one Mississippi, two Mississippi" before setting the hook on the next fish that rose to the fly, and soon he began getting results. That's right; he was wearing overalls, missing his front teeth, and hauling in one catfish after another.

Actually, this hesitation trick worked and he nailed a nice cutthroat a while later, letting out a loud "Yes!" as the line tightened and the trout jumped from the water about fifteen feet from the shore.

John caught on quickly also, his small arms working hard to move the rod between the ten o'clock and two o'clock casting positions and laying down a fine cast. The trout didn't seem too interested in his fly, and when you're just seven, a minute without a strike seems like an eternity and you get fidgety and start looking around and not paying attention to the fly, and then you put the rod down and start tossing rocks into the water.

Eventually the kids told me to knock it off because I was scaring the fish away.

John hooked his first trout on a fly rod that morning. This came after he had been sternly cautioned by me not to shout out any obscenities unless the fish was eighteen inches or longer.

The late-spring day was warm and sunny as we fished in the shadow of majestic Pikes Peak, and I knew fly-fishing had grabbed them like it had grabbed me some three decades earlier. We walked slowly on the way back, enjoying the smell of the forest, the majestic scenery, and the memory of big trout rising to their flies.

Then someone reached for another handful of elk droppings and the only mature member of the group whacked him on the back of the hand with a long stick and said, "Don't even think about it!"

Sometimes Maggie really ticks me off.

CHAPTER 34

The Kids and Ol' Sonuvabitch

As my kids' interest and skill in fly-fishing increased, I started taking them farther and farther from home, to some of the great trout rivers of the West. I was unable to catch anything in any of those places, though, so the kids unhooked *their* fish and decided we should go someplace "where Daddy can catch something, too." Then they'd laugh.

The ungrateful little @#$%^&s.

So in the early summer of 2001 we packed up the 1989 Chevy Suburban and headed for Taylor Reservoir, just north of Gunnison, Colorado, for a week of camping and fly-fishing along the shoreline where we'd caught many trout over the years. Taylor is about a four-hour drive from our home and we made ten stops along the way.

"I have to go to the bathroom!"

Twenty minutes later: "I have to go to the bathroom again!"

And again. And again.

It was infuriating.

Especially when Maggie yelled, "Geez, Dad, we want to go fishing. You should have your prostate gland checked."

Actually, the frequent stops were mainly for gasoline because someone at the fine General Motors Corp. decided years ago that it would be funny to make a vehicle that gets two miles to the gallon. Sometimes, as I drive around in my Suburban, crowds of Saudi Arabian-Americans stand on the sidewalks and cheer as I roar by, all of them waving, many with tears of joy streaming down their cheeks as they scream, *"Alulla Guccha!"*—which means "Thanks to you, even our camels wear Gucci loafers!"

Somehow we arrived at Taylor by midafternoon and began setting up camp. This became somewhat more difficult when we discovered that I had forgotten the tent poles in the garage. My kids, as you'd guess, were very understanding.

"Oh, way to go, Dad!"

"Way to show us about responsibility, Dad!"

"Way to be organized, Dad!"

"Now what are we going to do, Dad?"

(That fourth kid had just wandered over from the camp next door. The little $%^&*# is lucky he ran away because I was just about to smack him with the . . . empty . . . uh, nylon tent-pole bag.)

I managed to put up the tent without the poles, using a brilliantly engineered system involving what I estimated to be 143,500 feet of clothesline rope. When I was done, our tent stood proudly among the towering pines, fully prepared for any on-slaught nature might throw our way, unless the onslaught in-cluded something like rain or a breeze.

As a bonus, our campsite looked like, well, it looked like the web built by a hundred-foot-tall spider in that famous 1966 Japan-ese horror film *Gadtzaki*—which means "spider that spins clothes-line rope out of his butt, which has to be uncomfortable."

By early evening we were ready to head to the reservoir and rig up the fly rods, where I hoped to get another glimpse of the grandest trout I had ever seen, a stunningly huge and majestic brown trout that I'd seen at Taylor twice in the past few seasons, a fish so fine and so grand that I was left in awe.

I first saw him in the spring of 1998. I was wading the north shoreline, casting tiny emergers at rising rainbows in the clear water amid a submerged field of boulders and having a great time. And then he swam past, a behemoth of a fish, a trout I fig-ured might be thirty-five inches or longer, and as fat as a pig. A moment later he came to the surface and oinked, and I ran back to the shore, crying.

Okay, he didn't oink. I made that part up. But the fish that I guessed might weigh fifteen pounds or more turned when he got within ten feet of my waders and I saw the golden-yellow sides and the distinct spots on the brown trout, spots the size of silver dollars. I never even made a cast, settling that day for the simple pleasure of watching this gigantic trout—ruler of his domain, lord of his kingdom.

I named him with the first words that came out of my mouth when I saw him that day.

I call him "Sonuvabitch."

A year later I saw him again, I think. I was in a rented boat with my sons and their friend Spencer, moving toward the same boulder field from across the lake. When we got within a hundred feet of the spot, he came out of the water and I shouted "Sonuvabitch," as you do when you see an old friend. Spencer saw him, too, and while he didn't curse he did allow his mouth to open and a small bit of drool to run down his chin. Spencer is my friend Jim's son, and his father had obviously passed along this family trait: being speechless and drooling on yourself in disbelief when you actually see a fish.

"Did . . . did . . . you see that FISH?" Spencer shouted a few moments later, his eyes still as wide as cheap paper plates. (Sorry. I lost my saucers in the divorce, forcing me to come up with brand-new metaphors.)

"Oh yes, boy," I replied. "Indeed I did. I have seen this most imposing creature once before, this magnificent trout, and today we have encountered his lordship yet again. Rejoice, young man, in this moment!"

Although my boys and Spencer later insisted I'd only screamed "Sonuvabitch" and blew half a can of diet Pepsi out my nose.

Anyway, we would challenge the trout of Taylor once again on this late-summer afternoon, my kids and I casting to rising trout and catching five cutthroat along the rocky shoreline. We fished for only an hour or so on that first day of our camping trip before the sun faded behind the snowcapped peaks and we hurried back up the trail, me leading the way and my kids scurrying along behind in the gentle evening breeze. And as we moved through the golden light of dusk, four fly anglers filled with contentment, Nick spoke the hushed words that I can still hear today:

"I bet the tent blows over."

———

RICH TOSCHES

226

CHAPTER 35

Maggie the Cloven-Hoofed

With the clothesline rope holding up well in the face of this fierce three-mile-per-hour wind, the tent was not blown over. We cooked hot dogs and hamburgers and marshmallows over the fire that night, and then we slept, fifteen-year-old Maggie leading the way by saying good night and crawling headfirst into her sleeping bag.

The next morning was brisk and sunny and we caught a dozen or more trout before noon, rainbows and cutthroat that were feeding on a hatch of blue-winged olives. We'd take a break whenever any of us felt like it, which is, I think, the key to fishing with kids. We'd head back to the truck, drive to the store for a doughnut, or head back to the camp for a cup of hot chocolate.

John would use these breaks to feed the chipmunks around the camp, tossing sunflower seeds toward them and seeing how close he could get them to come. The first time he did this I began ranting and raving, sternly lecturing him about the dangers and telling him about the sign posted at the entrance of the campground warning us NOT to feed the chipmunks because of the great threat of injury, and that chipmunks had been seen foraging in this campground for more than a month.

Turns out the sign said BEARS, not CHIPMUNKS and we all had a good laugh.

Then I handed Nick a camera and pushed him out into the forest to get a picture of one of these bears—carrying on yet another proud Tosches family tradition, one passed from father to son for many generations. The lone break in this tradition came in the late 1800s, when little Nunzio Tosches was eaten. My great-grandfather said it happened near a dump.

The third day at Taylor would be our best. We'd found a point jutting out into the deeper water, and the trout were feeding close to the shore. This would allow the children—who did not yet have the technical casting savvy their father had long ago honed to a science—to make shorter, simpler casts and still reach the cruising fish. I explained all of that to them as I walked to the small, lone shrub behind me to retrieve the sixteenth fly I had snagged in its branches.

I rigged each of their rods with a large caddis that would float high on the water. Two feet beneath it would drift a small hare's ear, a common fly created with the fur of a rabbit, a fly that is relatively easy to tie. You know, if you can pry the rabbit out of the beagle's mouth.

Thirty feet offshore, large trout began a steady feeding pattern and the kids' excitement grew. Nick was the first to shout, his fly rod bending mightily as he set the hook after the dry fly had disappeared, tugged down by a trout that had taken the nymph below.

The fish ran left and then right and then Nick eased it onto the shore. He gently unhooked it, wet his hands before touching the fish so as not to rub away the delicate protective layer of slime on the fish, and then set it free. He had performed a difficult task, from detecting the strike and setting the hook to playing the sixteen-inch trout and releasing him, perfectly, as if he'd been doing it for twenty years.

This is the same kid who has a list of 435 excuses why his homework wasn't turned in on time. (No. 237: "A bat flew into my bedroom, lodged itself in my hair as bats will so often do, and I spent the entire night trying to get him out. Frankly, I'm lucky to be alive!")

John figured it out, too, making delicate casts and then watching intently as the big caddis bobbed in the gentle waves of the lake. When the fly disappeared, John would raise the rod and let out a hoot. "It's a big one!" he'd shout every time, although he knew none of these trout would make it into the prestigious "holy shit!" category. This was somewhat disappointing for the little guy.

A highlight came around 11 A.M. when Nick, staring intently at his large floating caddis and waiting for it to submerge, was greeted by an enormous splash as a very big trout rose from the water and slammed the dry fly. "Oh! Oh! Oh!" he yelped, setting the hook and stumbling backward as the fish ran toward him. Then it turned and fought doggedly—in the sense that at one point it came onto shore and bit Nick on the leg and then the fish sat down and licked its groin area.

Okay, it didn't, but the fish did fight hard and gave Nick all he could handle. But this kid was getting good, and with just the right amount of pressure he turned the battle and soon had the fish in the shallow water at his feet. It was a lake trout, the only one we'd catch on this trip, and stretched out to an impressive twenty-two inches.

But it was Maggie who turned in the all-star performance on this day. She had wandered away as we began fishing, seeking a bit of solitude, showing me that me she was starting to understand the heart of this special type of fishing. And quickly, she began hitting trout, the rod arcing overhead as a big rainbow or cutthroat slashed at the nymph, Maggie delicately setting the hook and quickly forcing the fish into submission. She would kneel at the water and remove the hook with a flick of her wrist, guide the trout back into the deeper water, stand for a moment and gaze out onto the water with a big smile, and then check the fly and begin casting again.

Watching Maggie fly-fish that day was sort of like looking at myself.

Except, of course, she's stunningly beautiful, doesn't have a potbelly or a giant behind, and has never, to my knowledge, shouted "Sonuvabitch!"

Although I have seen her shoot a soft drink out of her nose.

Late that afternoon, the wind and rain that had so perfectly stayed away for three days suddenly came hard, sweeping over the mountains. It made a mess of our campsite. Somehow, the clothesline rope didn't hold up as well as I'd imagined and the roof of the tent began collecting a bit of water, "bit" in this case meaning several hundred thousand gallons.

So we broke camp during a lull in the storm, packed everything back into the Suburban, and rented a cabin about a mile up the road, trading in the prospect of a night in wet sleeping bags for a warm, cozy cabin with real beds and a shower. As you might imagine, we were deeply saddened.

The storm passed at about 6 P.M. The kids had taken warm showers, changed into dry clothes, and were dancing in the cabin to a CD being played on a boom box that one of them had somehow hidden in the truck, probably under my six-foot-high mountain of clothesline rope. They were warm and happy and were not about to let that change.

So when I asked them if they wanted to go back out and fish the evening hatch, all three of my kids and their friend Spencer, who had stayed with us after his father had to return home, stared at me like . . . I don't know . . . like I had a bee on my forehead or something.

After I stopped screaming and got some ice onto the sting, I asked them if it would be okay if I went back to the lake to catch the evening hatch.

"Okay," Maggie said. "One hour. You've got one hour. Eight o'clock. Then come back and make us dinner. At eight o'clock! Right?"

I agreed and headed out the door for one hour of solitary fly-fishing. The fish dimpled the surface like raindrops, hundreds of rising trout on a mirror-slick surface, their snouts breaking the water and their dorsal fins emerging as they sipped at blue-winged olives. I had the perfect imitation, a No. 22, and began one of the greatest hours of my fly-fishing life.

I caught three trout on my first three casts, all fat, healthy rainbows between fifteen and eighteen inches. I'd rub the wetness from the fly, blow on it to dry the wings, and set it back down about thirty feet out. The wait generally lasted only a moment or two, with a fish rising in the slow, deliberate way to inhale the imitation.

Out in front stretched the Rocky Mountains, a golden light shimmering through the valleys as the summer sun set. And the trout just kept coming at the little blue-winged olive. I would occasionally glance down the shoreline and could see the tiny cabin, about a mile away. Even though Maggie was fifteen and was sickeningly responsible, I was a bit concerned because I knew that in that cabin were two things that should not be together:

Nick and matches.

From the age of two, Nick had been fascinated by matches and fire. He'd always ask if he could start the campfire, and then spend hours staring into the blaze and tossing things onto it. Sticks. Pinecones. Leaves. Charlie, my ex-mother-in-law's Yorkshire terrier.

Oops. That last one was just a lovely dream I had once.

But Nick had, indeed, been born with this love and fascination for fire, so I worried about him being in the cabin.

However, as we discussed earlier, God, in his infinite wisdom, had also given Nick a love of peeing on everything. I figured the two just sort of canceled each other out.

So I relaxed as I made a few more casts and then I checked my watch to see how close it was getting to the 8 P.M. deadline and saw that it wasn't close at all.

It was 9:20!

I snapped the fly off the leader, stuck it into my hat, reeled up the rest of the line, and sprinted across the gravel point. At about nine thousand feet in the Rockies, sprinting up a steep hillside isn't all that much fun in the sense that it often makes you throw up. But sprint is what I did, realizing that I was going to be facing the Wrath of Maggie, which is, as her brothers will tell you, not something you should take lightly.

I flung myself and the fly rod into the truck and sent gravel spewing across the landscape as the tires spun and I headed for the cabin. I drove way too fast on the mountain road and screeched to a halt in front of the cabin, quickly going over the explanation I would offer for my tardiness. (I had settled on the bat-in-the-hair thing, and thought I would dazzle them further by using the word "guano.")

I never got the chance. On the other side of the cabin door— the locked cabin door—stood Maggie, her brothers, and Spencer.

"If you want to come in," she shouted through the glass, "here's what we've decided you will do. You will run around the cabin two times, like a chicken. You will make loud clucking sounds. And you will flap your wings. Twice around the cabin."

Then we all laughed, my laughter echoing off the mountains and theirs muffled but still joyous inside our small cabin.

"You guys are too funny!" I shouted through my laughter. "A chicken! That's good. Let me in now and I'll start dinner."

Maggie's voice came back through the door like that of a fanged cacodemon from the Outer Darkness, the chilling sound of the archfiend of Gehenna himself, a voice booming from the fiery flames of Abaddon.

"Twice," the voice cracked. "Around the cabin. Like a chicken."

"Uh, no, really," I said, my voice wavering now, a forced half grin on my face. "In. Me. Start dinner. Eat now?"

"Flap your wings!" the voice of Beelzebub boomed from inside the cabin.

And the next thing I know I'm halfway around the back of the cabin, hopping, making really loud chicken sounds, my hands tucked into my armpits and my elbows flapping like, well, like a $%^&*@ chicken!

I was forty-five years old!

The kids followed me from inside, running from window to window to make sure I was clucking and hopping, their laughter filling the cabin. I got back to the door in about thirty seconds, paused, looked in at the glaring face of Maggie the Cloven-Hoofed, and just kept going, clucking and hopping and flapping my way around the outside of the cabin for the second time, which was just like the first lap except for the elderly couple who had now moved out onto the front porch of their cabin about fifteen feet from ours and were, well, "staring" is a good word.

"Are . . . are you okay?" the older man asked, his head cocked to one side like he'd never seen a middle-aged man racing around in the dark behaving like poultry.

"Oh yeah," I said, the stupid half grin reappearing on my face. "It's just my kids . . . inside the cabin . . . I fished too late . . . big hatch . . . kids won't let me in. Ha-ha."

As I talked to them and tried to explain the whole thing I realized that I had not stopped hopping. Up and down, up and down I hopped, just feet away from the startled couple.

Oh, and I was still flapping my "wings."

I couldn't think of anything else I could possibly say to the couple—I offered a weak "good night"—and I turned and then hopped and flapped my way off into the darkness around the corner of our cabin.

———

When I got back to the door, Maggie was smiling. "Did we learn a lesson?" she asked.

I was gasping for breath and I was shivering and I said that I had, and that I'd never fish too long ever again. And then my daughter let me in.

When we got home the next day we were still smiling about the chicken incident. After putting away the wet tent and the clothesline rope, I went inside and spent two hours putting old photographs—little Maggie taking her first bath, little Maggie having her diapers changed, little Maggie stumbling naked into the backyard on her first birthday—into an album.

And labeled it: "Show to boyfriends."

CHAPTER 36

A Tear and a Long-Tail Deer

One of the thousand special streams in Colorado is called the Williams Fork, a tributary of the Colorado River. It is a place of towering cottonwood trees and willow-lined banks and rolling hills filled with deer and elk, all tucked beneath a high plain of sagebrush that seems to roll on forever.

In October of 2001 I found myself crouched near the Williams Fork with Nick and John, miles from the nearest dirt road and huddled beneath the low branches of an enormous spruce tree as an autumn storm with snow and sleet and pounding wind battered the Rockies.

It was part of my annual elk-hunting trip, which had over the years become about 10 percent elk hunting and 90 percent fly-fishing. I'd hunt for a day and then put away the gun and take out the fly rod and begin a four-day adventure, fly-fishing alone from dawn till dusk.

But this year, for the first time, my sons would come along. I shot an elk, too. Nick and I dragged it out, about a mile, mostly downhill, and then collapsed. John had sat on a rock about twenty feet from the animal, at the age of nine not yet interested in the glamorous field-dressing aspect of hunting.

And the next day, with the elk hanging in the camp and the hard work completed, we went fly-fishing. The walk from the truck across the sage plain and down to the Williams Fork had taken most of an hour, and now, twenty feet from the water, we huddled under the spruce tree. Nick was shivering badly, complaining about the cold and the sideways sleet and saying that he felt weak. So I thought I'd take his mind off things by telling the lovely tale of the ill-fated Donner Party ("A long time ago in California, on a day just like this . . .") and the interesting way some members of the party managed to stay alive.

(I don't want to give away the ending for those of you who've not read about that exciting expedition, but I will give you one of their menu entrées: "Fillet of Saul.")

Anyway, telling the story was a good idea. When I finished, Nick said he was a lot warmer, felt much stronger than he had a few moments earlier. He even began whistling.

John was quiet and passed the time by tapping a stick rhythmically against the tree's trunk and casting an occasional glance at the meaty part of his brother's leg.

It was cold under that tree, despite the thick pine cover. The wind howled and the rain dripped from the branches onto us. But then the storm broke. The wind died and the sun poked out from the fast-moving clouds, and suddenly a cold, nasty, miserable day showed some promise.

We rigged our fly rods and headed through the willows to the river.

Brown trout of bragging size vaulted from the water, their red spots glistening in the sun before they came back down with frightening splashes, which caused one of us to swear. The boys had limited swearing privileges on this their first elk-hunting trip. I'd also taken them out of school for three days after both had knocked out some pretty good grades in the fall quarter.

I had thought I'd wait longer to introduce them to elk hunting. Some of my friends had already brought their sons, but with Nick and John at twelve and nine I figured there was plenty of time. But then September 11 came.

And by October, well, it just seemed like the right time to bring them a bit deeper into a world of smelly cabins and wood-burning stoves and long walks along rivers. And out of a world that was filled with images of hijacked airliners crashing into skyscrapers. And war. And anthrax.

So we loped along on the sagebrush plateau and then headed down the trail to the Williams Fork, where we shuffled through the fallen leaves. Once, we stopped to watch a white-tailed deer bound up a ridge to our left, pausing for a moment before she disappeared into the woods. I told Nick and John that the whitetail is common in the Eastern United States but somewhat rare in the

West, and that they have a much longer tail than our mule deer. They just kept walking. I wasn't sure they were listening.

We walked for another fifteen minutes or so, the stream rushing alongside our feet, and then John stopped, looked at me, and said, "Dad, do you think we'll see any more *long*-tail deer?"

Soon we settled near the big spruce and alongside a pool where a beaver dam had collapsed, a large structure of some fifty feet that had now given way in the middle. In the pool were a hundred or more big brown trout, I guessed, dozens and dozens of them rising at small insects and others vaulting clear of the water in eye-popping shows. It was the spawning season, so I talked to the boys about fishing clean and not injuring the trout, keeping our feet mostly on the bank so we wouldn't step on any of the beds.

And we caught trout. Oh, did we catch trout! A hatch of small duns had the big browns on a binge.

And Nick and John had this club in their bag, making gentle casts and letting the No. 20 duns float back to a spot where a trout was steadily rising. Their screams echoed through the canyon as I stood behind them, moving in to pop the tiny hooks free when the fish came in, Nick and John pausing only for a moment to watch the fish return to the pool before they cast again and again, nailing perhaps ten or twelve of the big fish. Yellow aspen leaves floated by on the river, the air turned warm, and geese flew overhead.

We released all of the trout and then began the long walk back to the truck. For about a mile none of us spoke. Then Nick stopped, looked around, and said, "Dad, this is great. Thanks."

I stayed ahead of them for the next mile, moving along in part because I knew the darkness was coming but mostly because I didn't want them to see the tears on their old man's face.

Two days later we were back home, back in a different world, a world of war, a world in which people were afraid to open their mail because they might inhale anthrax.

I hope my kids always remember which one is the real world.

CHAPTER 37

Undimmed by Human Tears

I'd like to tell a final story about
North Catamount Reservoir. It will
not be a funny story. (Here many of
you are asking, "And how does that make it different
from the rest of the book?")

Anyway, it's about a fishing excursion that I
made a few days after the terrorist attack on the
World Trade Center in New York and the Pentagon
in Washington in September of 2001. I needed to
get away. From the TV. From the newspapers. From
the heartache. I tried to get away from an America
that was hurt, saddened to the soul by the loss of

———

thousands of mothers and fathers, sisters and brothers, and children.

So I grabbed my fly rod.

It's what I always do when I need to leave the world for a while. I've fly-fished through the deaths of friends. I fly-fished through a divorce, too. (The settlement went well: I got to keep one hip boot and half of my lucky hat.)

So on that day when the world became too sad, I decided I'd walk the shoreline of a lake near my home high in the Rocky Mountains. I wanted to forget. But on this day that I wanted to forget the sorrow, I had chosen the wrong lake. And the wrong mountain. I picked North Catamount.

On the side of Pikes Peak.

The same Pikes Peak where, in 1893, Katharine Lee Bates sat down and wrote "America the Beautiful."

I knew I'd made a mistake when I came to the stand of yellow aspens where, a few Septembers earlier, my children and I stopped to gather leaves and to rub the white "paint" from the bark onto our faces. The Indians did that, my little Maggie told me that day, to keep from getting sunburned.

I thought of that day, and I smiled.

But I stopped when I remembered that the next day, a not-so-little-anymore daughter would be bused to and from her high school, which is located inside the boundary of the United States Air Force Academy, which, in the wake of the attack, was cloaked in the highest level of security.

They said that week that we were at war.

I eventually got to my spot near a cove on the lake, and as I made the first few casts I looked up at the peak towering just over my head.

RICH TOSCHES

O beautiful for patriot's dream
That sees beyond the years.
Thine alabaster cities' gleam,
Undimmed by human tears.

I wondered if Katharine Lee Bates could ever have imagined that many tears.

The sun climbed higher and a rainbow trout rose to my fly. As I released him I thought about my father, who despite not knowing fly-fishing from flypaper, saw his son's eagerness and bought him a fly rod when he was twelve. And at some point, as I stood high in the Rockies, it occurred to me that someday we'd all climb out of that hole we were in during that horrific time, and that life would go on. And that I'd get to spend another day fly-fishing with my kids.

And that two thousand miles away, they may have hit the World Trade Center and they may have hit the Pentagon.

But they had missed America.

And that on this brilliant September day, I hadn't chosen the wrong mountain at all.